Learn from Home
WORKBOOK

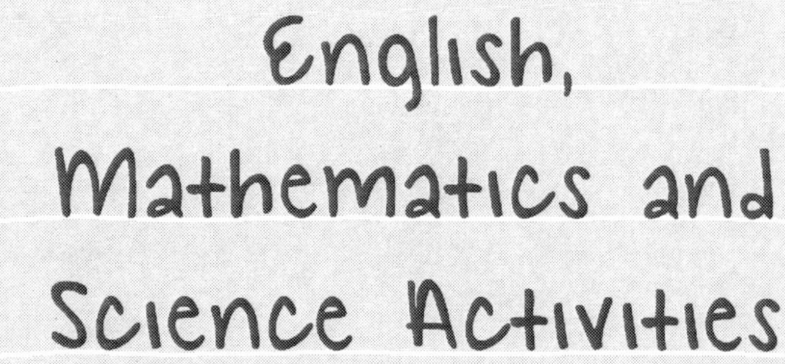

Learn from Home – Workbook 4

Published by Prim-Ed Publishing 2020
Copyright© R.I.C. Publications® 2020

ISBN 978-1-912760-64-0

PR–8491

Titles available in this series:

Learn from Home–Workbook 1 – *1st Class/Year 1*
Learn from Home–Workbook 2 – *2nd Class/Year 2*
Learn from Home–Workbook 3 – *3rd Class/Year 3*
Learn from Home–Workbook 4 – *4th Class/Year 4*
Learn from Home–Workbook 5 – *5th Class/Year 5*
Learn from Home–Workbook 6 – *6th Class/Year 6*

Prim-Ed Publishing
Marshmeadows
New Ross
Co. Wexford
Y34 TA46
Ireland

Ireland: (051) 440075

UK: +44 (0) 20 3773 9630

Email: sales@prim-ed.com

Internet websites

In some cases, websites or specific URLs may be recommended. While these are checked and rechecked at the time of publication the publisher has no control over any subsequent changes which may be made to webpages. It is *strongly* recommended that the class teacher checks *all* URLs before allowing pupils to access them.

View all pages online

Email address: sales@prim-ed.com

www.prim-ed.com

CONTENTS PAGE

WEEK 1

ENGLISH

MATHEMATICS

SCIENCE

The Myth of the Giant's Causeway – 1

Read this version of the myth.

Long ago, when giants roamed the earth, the Irish giant Finn McCool, who was tired of his Scottish enemy across the sea, decided to do something about it. The giants would often taunt and insult each other across the water and one day Finn became so angry that he gathered up a large clump of earth and hurled it towards his rival. However, the clump missed its target, instead becoming the Isle of Man and leaving the enormous hole to become the great Lough Neagh (the largest lake in the British Isles).

After another occasion of jeering and tormenting, Finn came up with a plan. He gathered many large stone columns and heaved them into the sea. The stones landed side by side, creating a stone bridge, or causeway, between the two nations.

Soon after, Finn spotted his arch nemesis Benandonner, The Red Man, and shouted a challenge to him. 'Come and fight me and let's settle this once and for all!' Finn stayed to watch The Red Man approach and soon realised his great mistake! As Benandonner came closer, Finn realised just how huge the giant really was ... much bigger than him! Finn skedaddled home quick smart to tell his wife of his grave mistake. By the time he'd finished explaining they could hear the thunderous footsteps of the approaching giant and feel the floor quaking beneath them.

At the giant's booming knock on their door, Finn's wife Oonagh hatched a plan. She shoved Finn into the giant-sized bath, covered him in blankets and placed a baby's toy in his hand and a bonnet on his head. She rushed to the door and greeted Benandonner explaining, 'What a pity you've just missed Finn! He's away hunting deer. Come in for a rest after your journey and you can wait for his return.' Oonagh offered the giant a drink while he waited.

When he had finished, Oonagh loudly asked him if he'd like to see their baby while he waited for Finn. Not knowing what else to do, Benandonner reluctantly agreed and followed Oonagh's lead through the house.

When she opened the door she greeted her baby, who was sucking his thumb and cooing under the blanket in the bathtub (of course it was Finn McCool himself). The giant Benandonner quickly excused himself, saying he needed to get some air. 'Och', thought the giant, 'if that's the size of the wee laddie I'd hate to see his father. I'll not wait for him to return!' And with that thought, Benandonner broke into a run all the way back home to Scotland. When he heard the giant run off, Finn thanked his quick-thinking and clever wife. As Benandonner thundered back across the causeway he made sure to tear the blocks up to prevent Finn from ever following him.

The remnants of the Giant's Causeway can be seen to this day on the north-east coast of Northern Ireland (County Antrim).

My learning log	When I read this myth, I could read:	☐ all of it.	☐ most of it.	☐ parts of it.

The Myth of the Giant's Causeway – 2

1. This myth was told to:

   (a) make people laugh.

   (b) explain a natural feature.

   (c) warn children of danger.

2. Which two countries are mentioned in the text?

   ____

3. At what point in the story did Finn regret building the causeway? Explain why.

   ____

   ____

4. How did Finn and his wife Oonagh trick the giant Benandonner?

   ____

   ____

5. Do you think this story tells the real version of how the causeway came to be there? Give reasons for your response.

   ____

   ____

6. Use the text to help you describe the three characters. Think about their physical traits as well as their personalities.

   (a) Finn McCool: ____

   (b) Benandonner: ____

   (c) Oonagh: ____

7. Rewrite the phrase 'Finn spotted his arch nemesis Benandonner' in your own words.

   ____

   ____

My learning log	While doing these activities:		
	I found Q ______ easy.	I found Q ______ challenging.	I found Q ______ interesting.

The Myth of the Giant's Causeway – 3

1. Write a Standard English definition for each of these Scottish words. Use the text to help you.

   (a) wee _____________   (b) laddie _____________   (c) och _____________

2. Write the root words for these words from the text.

   (a) thunderous _____________   (b) approaching _____________

   (c) reluctantly _____________   (d) realised _____________

   (e) sucking _____________   (f) quickly _____________

3. Find and write words in the text that come from:

   (a) the Latin word 'columna' meaning 'pillar'.   _____________

   (b) the Old English word 'wif' meaning 'woman'.   _____________

   (c) the Old French word 'journee' meaning a 'day's travel'. _____________

4. (a) Find two words in the text with the suffix '-ous'.

   _________________________   _________________________

   (b) Write a sentence using both of these words.

   ____

   ____

5. Use a dictionary to write the meanings of these words.

   (a) jeer ____

   (b) reluctant ____

   (c) prevent ____

6. Write synonyms from the text for the words below.

   (a) ocean _________   (b) weary _________   (c) duvet _________

   (d) rock _________   (e) threw _________   (f) sprint _________

   (g) hat _________   (h) beverage _________   (i) error _________

My learning log	*Colour:*	I recognise / can't recognise the roots of words.
		I can / can't use a dictionary to write word definitions.
		I understand / need more practice on synonyms.

Whuppity Stoorie – 1

Read this Scottish version of the fairy tale.

There once was a woman, the goodwife of Kittlerumpit, who was facing some hard times. She was all alone with her infant child as her husband had gone out one day and never returned. To make matters even worse, her only hope of making a living, the pregnant sow she had in the yard, was sick and close to death.

The goodwife became distraught as she worried for her future and the future of her baby. She sat by her cottage with the child in her arms and began to cry and wail in despair.

Looking up for just a moment, the goodwife noticed a strange figure approaching. The figure came closer and the goodwife could make out that it was a small and crooked old woman, very smartly dressed in a green, velvet frock and a crisp, white apron. The goodwife also took note of the large staff the woman used to help her walk. As she approached, the woman spoke to the goodwife.

'Now save your tales of woe. I know all about your husband and your sow and I'm here to tell you I can heal her. Would you like that?'

'Oh yes please!' replied the goodwife gratefully. 'It'll mean so much to myself and the wee one.'

'Aye, very well then. But tell me, what'll you give me in return, I ask?'

'Oh anything, anything at all', the foolish woman responded.

With a quick chant and a sprinkle of magic, the pig was up and eating in no time.

The goodwife felt so relieved and asked the woman, 'How will I ever repay you?'

'Well there's just one thing I'll ask for, your wee bairn.' At the goodwife's cries of protest the woman explained. 'Under the law I live by, I cannot take him until the third day, and not then, if by chance you can tell me my right name.' And off she went with a smug smile.

The goodwife held her baby so tightly and wept the entire first day. On the second day she decided to walk with the wee one in the woods. On and on she walked in a daze until she heard a voice. She spotted the very woman through the trees spinning away on her wheel and babbling to herself.

'Ah a new baby old Whuppity Stoorie'll have at sun up tomorrow!' she said, full of delight.

At that the woman rushed home with a much lighter heart, to rest up before the spiteful fairy returned to claim her beloved son.

The goodwife was a lighthearted woman normally and she decided to play a trick on the ugly old fairy. When she came to collect the baby, the goodwife kept up her crying and wailing and only at the very last moment did she speak the name 'Whuppity Stoorie'. At that, the shocked fairy jumped a mile into the air and when she landed she whirled around and ran off screaming with furious rage. The goodwife laughed and hugged and kissed her baby joyously.

My learning log	When I read this fairy tale, I could read:	☐ all of it. ☐ most of it. ☐ parts of it.

Whuppity Stoorie – 2

1. What do you think happened to the goodwife after this story?

____

____

2. What do you think happened to Whuppity Stoorie?

____

____

3. Use a dictionary to define the word 'distraught'.

____

4. Explain why the woman became so worried about the future of herself and her baby.

____

____

5. Explain how these phrases can help the reader predict what might happen in the story.

(a) … anything at all', the foolish woman responded.

____

(b) … and not then, if by chance you can tell me my right name.

____

6. Write a chant the fairy might have said to make the sow well again.

____

____

7. Explain the meanings of the phrases.

(a) facing hard times _______________________________

(b) tales of woe _______________________________

(c) lighter heart _______________________________

My learning log	While doing these activities:		
	I found Q _____ easy.	I found Q _____ challenging.	I found Q _____ interesting.

Whuppity Stoorie – 3

1. The fairy had a 'smug' smile. This means:

(a) uncertain ☐ (b) superior ☐ (c) lopsided ☐

2. Use a dictionary to write the meanings of these words.

(a) staff ____

(b) figure ____

(c) wail ____

3. (a) Circle the words ending with the suffix '-ly'.

> normally   tightly   only   gratefully   smartly   ugly

(b) Find and write one more word from the text with the suffix '-ly'.

____

(c) Write a sentence using two of these '-ly' words.

____

4. Write homophones from the text for the words below.

(a) whale _________ (b) herd _________ (c) write _________

(d) sun _________ (e) their _________ (f) sum _________

(g) heel _________ (h) threw _________ (i) four _________

5. Find four compound words in the text. The first letter is given.

(a) g_________ (b) a_________

(c) m_________ (d) l_________

6. Write antonyms from the text for the words below.

(a) easy _________ (b) pretty _________ (c) heavier _________

(d) past _________ (e) young _________ (f) scruffily _________

(g) slow _________ (h) wife _________ (i) better _________

My learning log	Colour:	I can / can't use a dictionary to write word definitions.
		I can / can't recognise compound words.
		I understand / need more practice on antonyms.

Common and proper nouns

Proper nouns are words that start with capital letters to name particular people, places or things.

Common nouns name general things, people, places, feelings and ideas.

1. Read these fairytale newspaper headlines.

Cinderella loses slipper … again!

Princess of Hapland points finger of blame at the Three Blind Mice to explain disappearing shoes.

Fire-breathing newt escapes!

'I had no idea I left the gate open', says shocked king.

Fluffy the Dragon in rescue disaster

Police become suspicious as sheep are 'accidentally' barbecued during mouth-to-mouth resuscitation.

2. Write the proper nouns and common nouns from each headline under the correct heading in the table below. Add some other nouns to the table that you think might be included in the rest of the articles.

Proper nouns	Common nouns

3. There are four four-letter nouns in the second newspaper report. Write them below, then try to fit them into this square puzzle. Each word must go both across and down.

- ______________________________
- ______________________________
- ______________________________
- ______________________________

Collective and abstract nouns

Abstract nouns are words that name things we cannot touch, smell, see, taste or hear. They are often the names of feelings, events and ideas.

John's **friendship** with the alien brought new **information**, **technology** and **knowledge** to the people of Earth. In return, the alien had, for the first **time**, experienced **humour** and **happiness**. It was John's **belief** that their **friendship** would create **peace** between the two planets.

1. Write any two abstract nouns from the paragraph above and draw a symbol to represent each.

2. For each of the concrete nouns below, write an abstract noun (idea or feeling) to show what each means to you or what feelings it gives you;

   e.g. My teacher's *smile* means *approval* to me.

   (a) A puppy **dog** means _______________________

   (b) A good **joke** means _______________________

   (c) A shiny **trophy** means _______________________

   (d) A green **apple** means _______________________

Collective nouns are words that name groups of people, places and things. For example, 'team' is the collective noun for a group of people doing something (usually playing a game) together.

3. Rearrange the boxes with pairs of letters to find the collective nouns. Don't change the order of the letters inside the boxes.

   (a) a | st | ho | of angels _______________________

   (b) an | ch | or | ra | est | of musicians _______________________

   (c) a | ng | ri | st | of ponies _______________________

   (d) a | er | qu | iv | of arrows _______________________

   (e) a | le | ga | gg | of geese _______________________

  Learn from Home Workbook 4   978-1-912760-64-0   www.prim-ed.com   Prim-Ed Publishing

Trefin

Ceridwen was a witch who lived many, many years ago in the wild, rugged mountains of North Wales. She had a beautiful daughter, Cerys, and an ugly son, Avagon. Ceridwen decided to brew for her son a magic potion of Inspiration and Knowledge. This would give him the power to know all the secrets of the future and people would think he was clever instead of laughing at his ugliness.

Gwyn, a young servant boy, stirred the boiling mixture every day until, at last, just three powerful drops of the magic potion remained. These precious drops contained all the magic and wisdom Avagon would ever need. But on the final day, the drops splashed on to Gwyn's hand and scalded him. He licked his hand to soothe the pain and immediately saw all the secrets of the past, present and future.

Gwyn fled in terror.

Ceridwen chased after the frightened boy, determined to kill him. Gwyn changed into a swift hare, but she changed into a sprinting greyhound and ran even faster. He dived into a river and became a darting fish, but she turned into a slinky otter and still pursued him. He took flight and became a scurrying fieldmouse, but Ceridwen became a preying owl. He dived into a field of wheat and became a golden grain. Ceridwen became a pecking hen and swallowed the golden grain.

Ceridwen carried the grain for nine months until Gwyn was born again. She had planned to kill him but he was so beautiful, she could not. Instead, she wrapped him in blankets and cast him adrift on the sea in a small boat, to die or survive.

The child was rescued by a prince named Ethen, who called him Trefin. Trefin lived in the prince's court. Having tasted the drops of Inspiration and Knowledge, he became the greatest poet in all Wales, even though he was still a child.

Use the narrative on page 3 to answer the questions.

1. Title

What is the title of the story?

2. Orientation

(a) Where is the story set?

____

(b) Is the story set in the

present? ☐

past? ☐

future? ☐

(c) Which main character is introduced in the first paragraph?

____

(d) Why did Ceridwen want to make a special brew?

____

3. Complication and events

(a) What went wrong with Ceridwen's plan?

____

____

Descriptive language is used to improve the quality of a narrative text.

(b) From the text, write three adjectives and the nouns they are describing.

adjective	noun

4. Resolution

(a) At first, how did Ceridwen try to resolve the complication?

____

(b) How did Ceridwen eventually solve the problem?

____

5. Conclusion

What became of Gwyn?

1. Plan an ancient myth.

Title

Orientation

Complication and events

Resolution

Conclusion

2. Write your narrative.

3. Edit your work.

The beach

Read the description.

glorious, white sand covered the ground like a jewel-studded carpit the hot sun, slowly moveing towards the horizon, caused each grain to sparkle like a diamond the ocean lay like a vast expanse of shiny, turquoise (clothe/cloth), glittering in the early evening (son/sun) the surf was active but not angre the next breaker rose like a curved wall as it travelled toowards the (shore/sure)

❶ Punctuation

(a) The description needs 5 capital letters and 5 full stops.

(b) Circle all the commas. How many are there? _______

❷ Spelling

(a) Circle the correct word in each bracket.

(b) Write the correct spelling of the 4 misspelt words.

_______________ _______________

_______________ _______________

❸ Grammar

Adjectives are used to describe nouns.

(a) Write the adjectives used to describe these nouns in the text.

(i) the sand _______________

(ii) the ocean _______________

(iii) the surf _______________

(iv) a wall _______________

(v) the evening _______________

❹ Vocabulary

*A simile compares one thing with another; e.g. He ran **like** the wind; **As** blind as a bat.*

(a) Underline then write the 4 similes in the text.

- _______________________________

  ____

- _______________________________

  ____

  ____

- _______________________________

  ____

- _______________________________

  ____

❺ Writing

Our sense of smell is very powerful in reminding us of a particular place.

(a) Using adjectives and similes, write a sentence to describe the smell of a place you know.

____

____

Elephants can fly!

Read the recount.

this morning, london's heathrow airport <u>was</u> the centre of a massive operation (two/too) fully grown indian elephants <u>were flown</u> in from mumbai, india as part of a worldwide breeding programme

the elephants, a young female named trisha and rajah, a ten-year-old (mail/male), <u>will be housed</u> in specially constructed compounds at london zoo they <u>will join</u> misha, a long-time resident and a favourite with the zoo's (many/meny) visitors

martin jones, the coordinator of the ambitious project, <u>told</u> reporters that the elephants, (which/witch) <u>travelled</u> in specially designed crates, (<u>flu/flew</u>) very well

❶ Punctuation

(a) The recount needs 17 capital letters (13 for proper nouns) and 5 full stops.

(b) Circle all the commas. How many are there? _______

(c) Circle the words with apostrophes.

(d) Why is there an apostrophe in these two words?

____

____

❷ Spelling

(a) Highlight the correct spelling of the words in brackets.

❸ Grammar

An apostrophe is used to show ownership. It goes after the owner(s); e.g. the lady's bag, the ladies' bags.

(a) Add apostrophes to show ownership.

(i) the elephants tails

(ii) the childrens visit

(iii) Trishas compound

(b) There are 7 verbs underlined in the text. Write each verb in the correct column according to its tense.

Past tense	Future tense

(c) Which tense was more often used?

____

❹ Writing

(a) How many paragraphs are there in this recount? _______

(b) What does the first paragraph explain?

____

____

____

How a thermometer works

Read the explanation.

a thermometer is a instrument used to measure heat _______________

thermometers are maid from a glass tube with a scale _______________
on the outside, and filled with a liquid, usualy mercury _______________

mercury is the liquid which is most ofen used, because it _______________
always changes in the same way, when the same tempature _______________
is applied it fills a glass bulb wich is connected to a thin sealed _______________
tube, also partially filed with mercury when the glass tube is _______________
warmed, the mercury expands and rises to the same piont in _______________
the tube whenever the same amownt of heat is applied _______________

thermometers are used for meny purposes, including _______________
medicine science and in cooking they play a important _______________
roll in our lives _______________

❶ Punctuation

(a) The explanation needs 7 capital letters, 7 full stops and 1 comma in the last paragraph.

❷ Spelling

(a) Underline the spelling mistake on each line of text and write the correction at the end of the line.

❸ Grammar

(a) Write the 3 plural nouns used in the text.

____

____

____

(b) Underline all the words following 'a' and 'an' in the text. List them below.

words following 'a'	words following 'an'

(c) Explain why it is sometimes necessary to write or say 'an' instead of 'a'.

____

____

COUNTING IN SIXES, SEVENS AND NINES

1. Fill in the missing numbers on the hundreds chart.

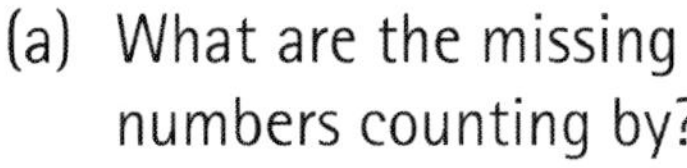

(a) What are the missing numbers counting by?

____

(b) What are the numbers with a triangle around them counting by?

____

(c) What are the circled numbers counting by?

____

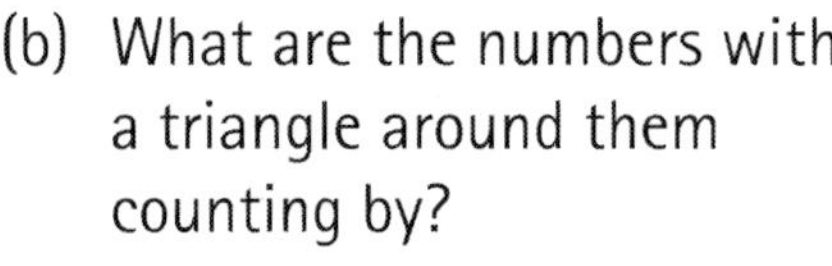

1	2	3	4	5		7	8	9	10
11		13	14	15	16	17		19	20
21	22	23		25	26	27	28	29	
31	32	33	34	35		37	38	39	40
41		43	44	45	46	47		49	50
51	52	53		55	56	57	58	59	
61	62	63	64	65		67	68	69	70
71		73	74	75	76	77		79	80
81	82	83		85	86	87	88	89	
91	92	93	94	95		97	98	99	100

2. Continue the number patterns.

(a) 0, 6, 12, 18, ______, ______, ______, ______, ______, ______, ______

(b) 0, 7, 14, 21, ______, ______, ______, ______, ______, ______, ______

(c) 0, 9, 18, 27, ______, ______, ______, ______, ______, ______, ______

(d) 90, 81, 72, 63, ______, ______, ______, ______, ______, ______, ______

(e) 60, 54, 48, 42, ______, ______, ______, ______, ______, ______

(f) 70, 63, 56, 49, ______, ______, ______, ______, ______, ______, ______

CHALLENGE

Which answers are in the following multiplication tables (to x10)?

(a) 6 and 7 ________

(b) 7 and 9 ________, ________

(c) 9 and 6 ________, ________ and ________

Objective   *Counts on and back in 6s, 7s and 9s.*

When a number is passed through the robot it is changed according to the rule programmed into the machine. For example, the following robot is programmed to multiply by 6.

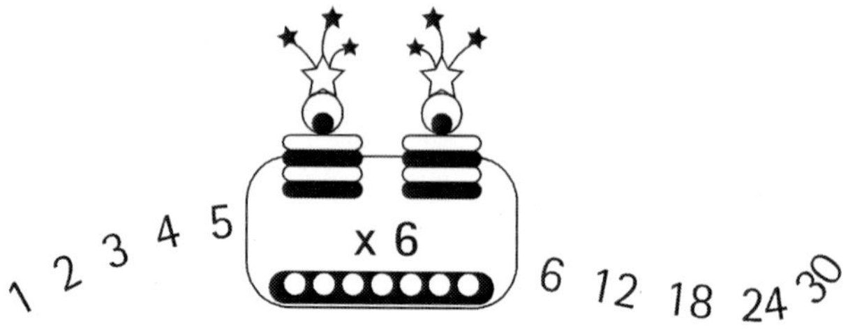

1 2 3 4 5 → × 6 → 6 12 18 24 30

1. Work out what each of the following robots do and write the program on the face.

(a) 1 2 3 4 5 → 2 4 6 8 10

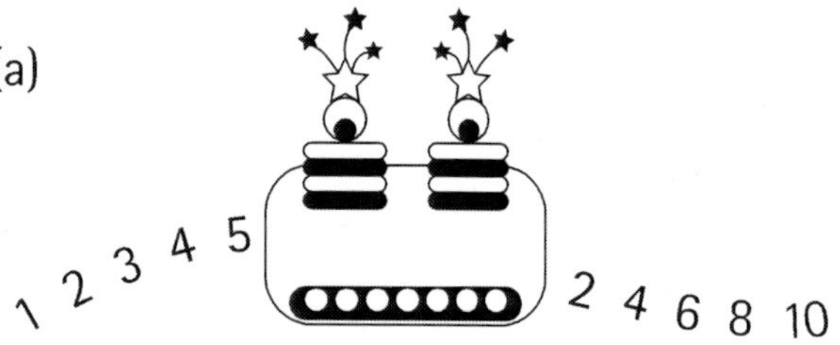

(b) 1 2 3 4 5 → 6 12 18 24 30

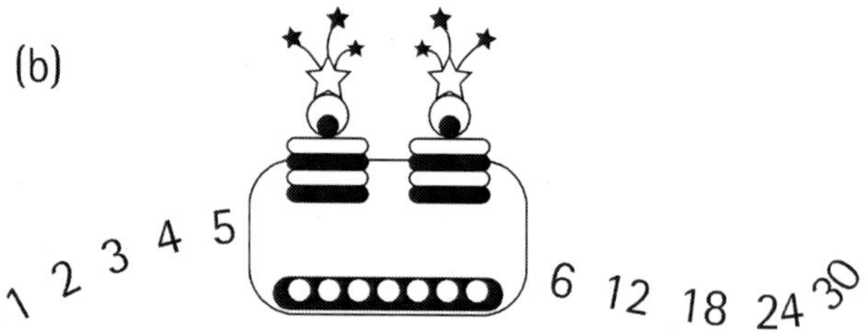

(c) 2 4 6 8 10 → 6 12 18 24 30

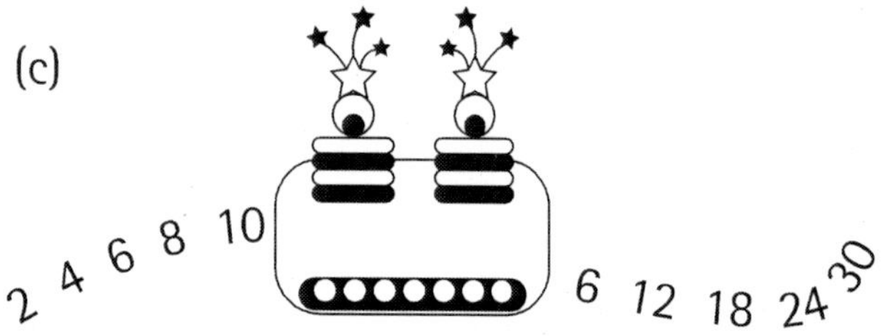

(d) 2 4 6 8 10 → 10 20 30 40 50

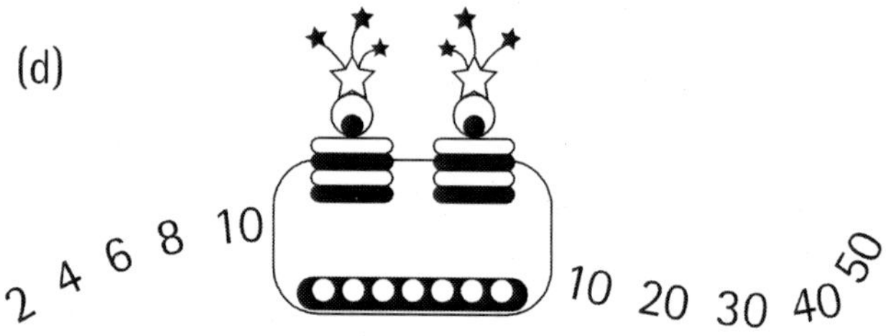

(e) 2 4 6 8 10 → 12 24 36 48 60

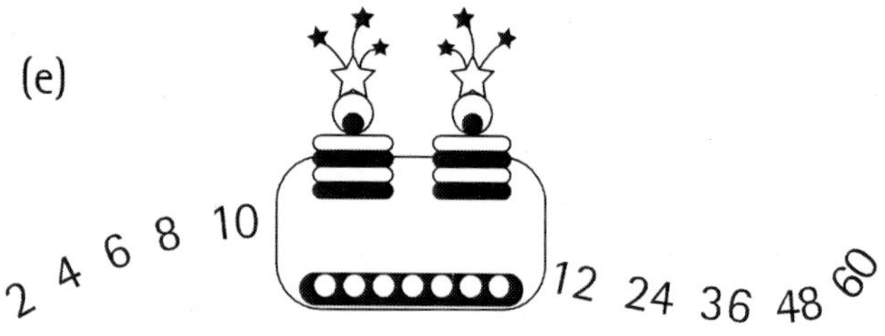

(f) 3 4 5 6 7 → 30 40 50 60 70

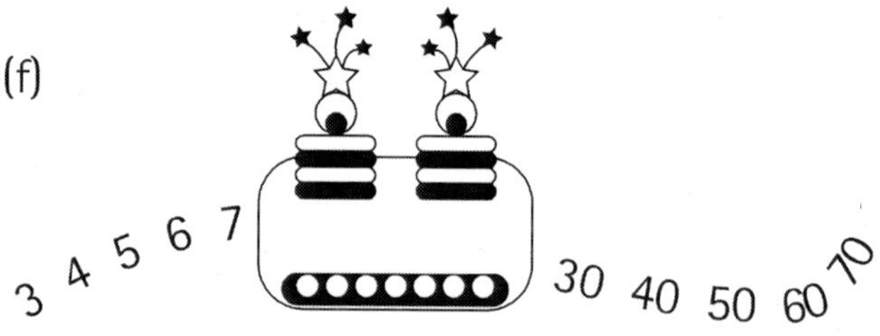

(g) 1 2 3 4 5 → 4 8 12 16 20

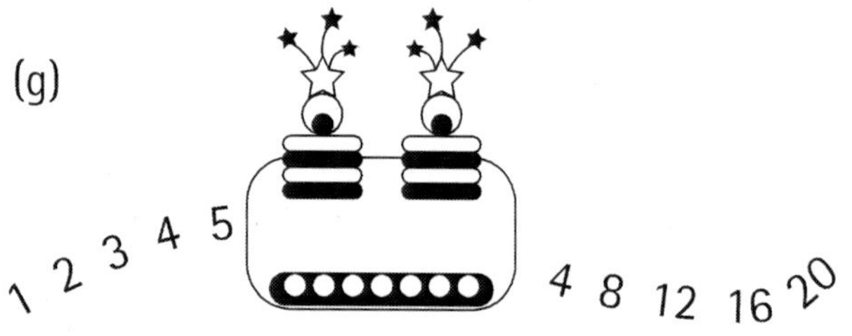

(h) 1 2 3 4 → 25 50 75 100

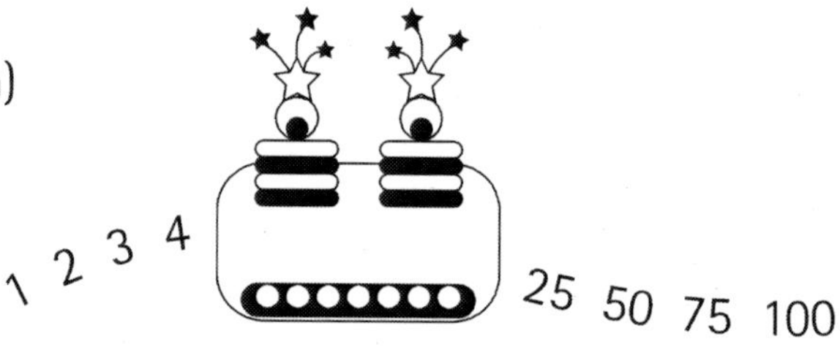

(i) 2 4 6 8 10 → 18 36 54 72 90

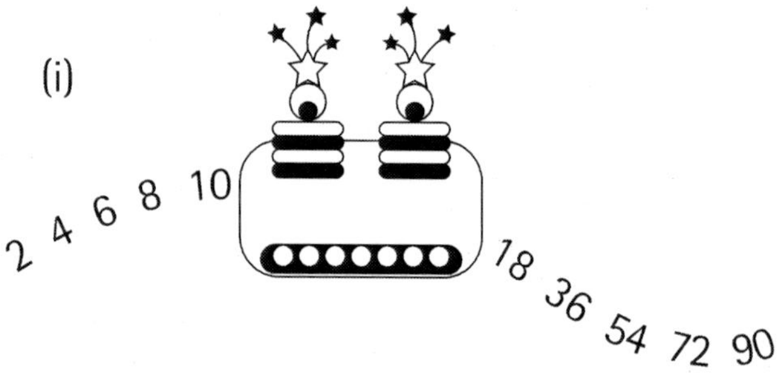

(j) 1 2 3 4 5 → 7 14 21 28 35

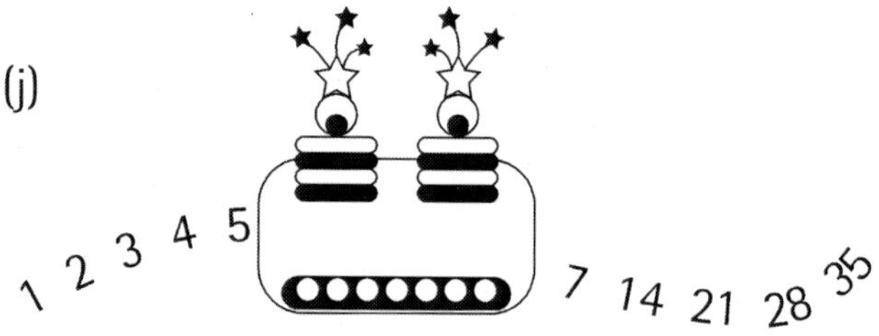

CHALLENGE

Write robot questions with missing functions. Give them to a friend to solve.
Remember to write the missing functions on a separate sheet of paper.

Objective *Solves multiplication number problems.*

EXPANDED COLUMN ADDITION

1. Use expanded column addition to solve these sums.

Example:	
38	
+ 25	
13	(Add the ones: 8 + 5)
50	(Add the tens: 20 + 30)
63	(Add the two answers: 13 + 50)

(a)
```
    2   4
+   3   7
```
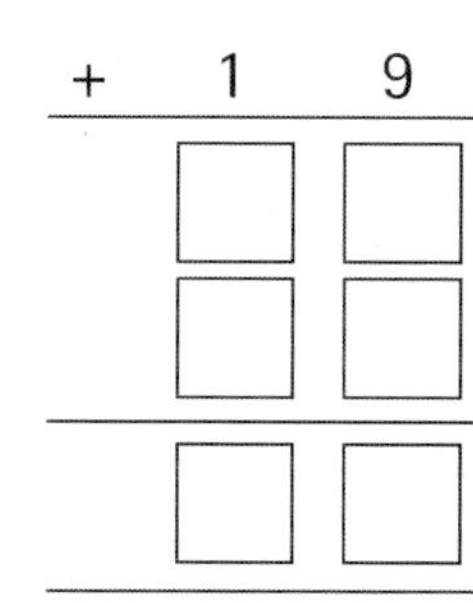

(b)
```
    4   6
+   1   9
```

(c)
```
  4   3
+ 5   1
```
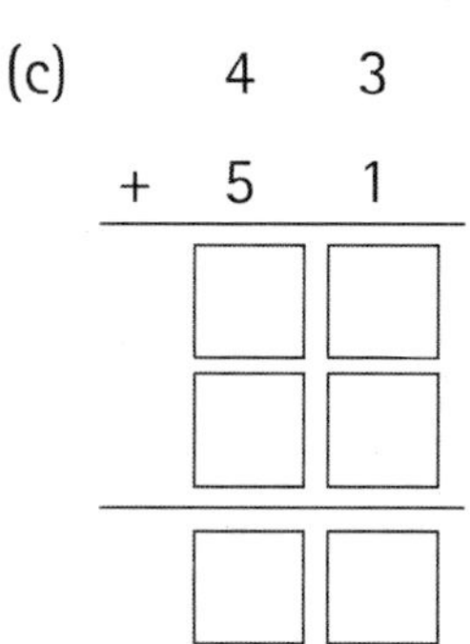

(d)
```
  6   9
+ 2   7
```
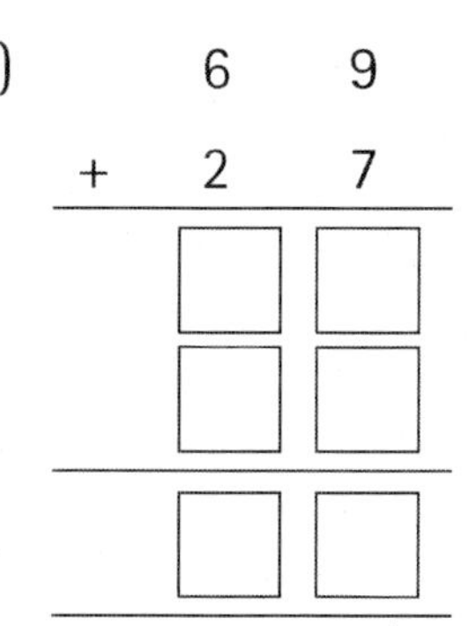

(e)
```
    3   4
+   9   3
```
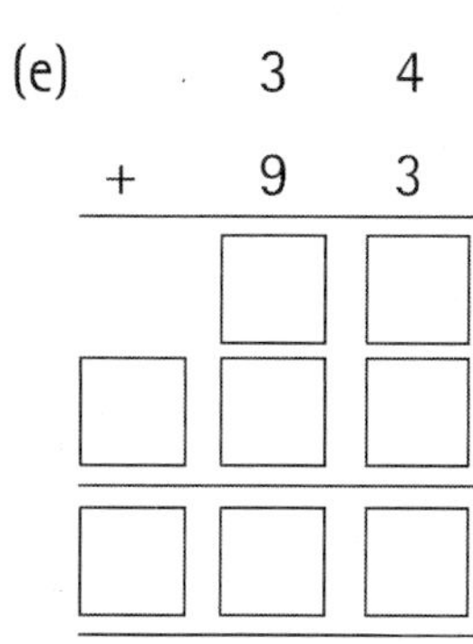

(f)
```
    5   3
+   7   6
```

2. Use expanded column addition to solve these sums.

Example:	
285	
+ 312	
7	(Add the ones: 5 + 2)
90	(Add the tens: 80 + 10)
500	(Add the hundreds: 200 + 300)
597	(Add the three answers: 7 + 90 + 500)

(a)
```
    2   4   1
+   3   5   6
```

(b)
```
    2   1   9
+   4   7   2
```

(c)
```
  2   2   8
+ 5   9   0
```

(d)
```
  3   8   5
+ 5   0   9
```

(e)
```
  5   9   4
+ 3   2   7
```
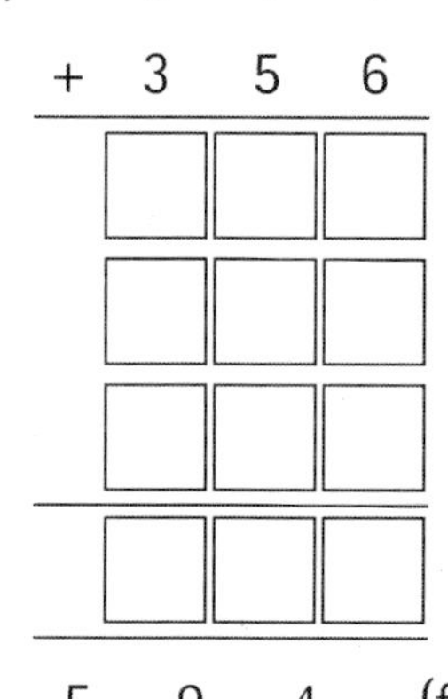

(f)
```
  9   2   8
+ 5   1   4
```
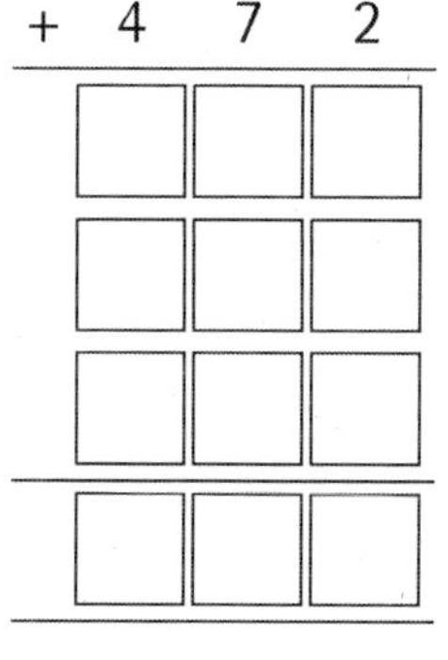

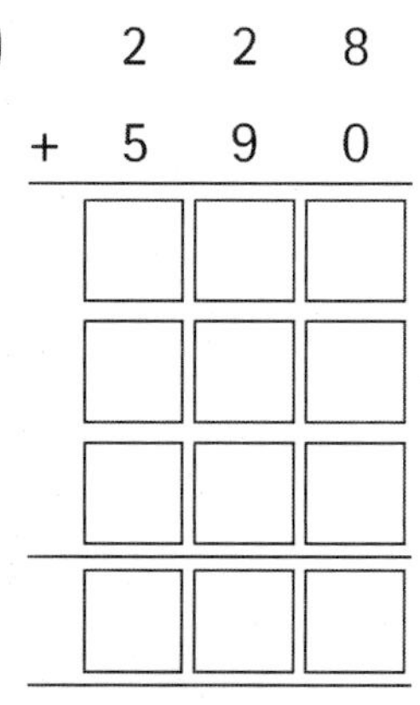
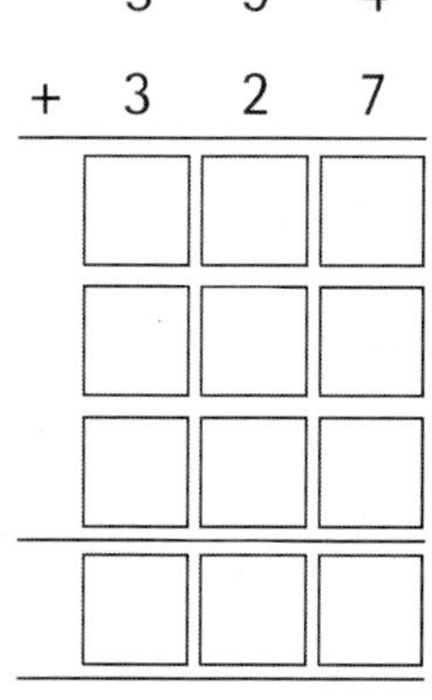

CHALLENGE

Solve these addition sums on the back of the sheet.

(a) 64 + 35   (b) 85 + 76   (c) 376 + 609   (d) 412 + 369

Objective   *Solves addition sums using expanded column addition.*

LENGTH AND DECIMALS

Length can be recorded using decimals;
for example, 1 m and 34 cm = 1.34 m.

1. Write these measurements in decimal numbers.

   (a) 1 m 25 cm = _______ m   (b) 2 m 13 cm = _______ m   (c) 4 m 30 cm = _______ m

   (d) 2 m 78 cm = _______ m   (e) 3 m 42 cm = _______ m   (f) 5 m 99 cm = _______ m

2. Write these decimals in metres and centimetres.

   (a) 3.10 m = _______ m _______ cm   (b) 1.80 m = _______ m _______ cm

   (c) 2.20 m = _______ m _______ cm   (d) 5.04 m = _______ m _______ cm

   (e) 7.20 m = _______ m _______ cm   (f) 4.10 m = _______ m _______ cm

3. These pupils' heights were recorded in centimetres. Write them in metres, using a decimal point.
   For example, 116 cm = 1.16 m

(a)	Lisa	– 118 cm =	_______ m
(b)	Clare	– 115 cm =	_______ m
(c)	Michael	– 120 cm =	_______ m
(d)	Lee	– 116 cm =	_______ m
(e)	John	– 122 cm =	_______ m
(f)	Sarah	– 112 cm =	_______ m
(g)	Ben	– 125 cm =	_______ m
(h)	Emma	– 119 cm =	_______ m

4. There are 10 mm in 1 cm. Write these measurements in decimal numbers.

   (a) 15 mm = ___*1.5*___ cm

   (b) 19 mm = _______ cm

   (c) 32 mm = _______ cm

   (d) 48 mm = _______ cm

   (e) 65 mm = _______ cm

   (f) 96 mm = _______ cm

   (g) 112 mm = _______ cm

   (h) 134 mm = _______ cm

CHALLENGE

On the back of the sheet, measure and record the height of five of your friends in metres and centimetres, using decimal points. Who is the tallest? Write their names in order from tallest to shortest.

Objective   *Demonstrates understanding of the use of decimals in measurement units.*

EQUIVALENT LENGTHS

1. Match the units of measure to the correct abbreviation.

(a) millimetres •   • cm

(b) centimetres •   • km

(c) metres •   • mm

(d) kilometres •   • m

2. Answer these statements.

(a) There are _______ millimetres in 1 centimetre.

(b) There are _______ centimetres in 1 metre.   (c) There are _______ metres in 1 kilometre.

3. (a) Write the four units of length in order of size, from smallest to largest.

metres	centimetres	kilometres	millimetres

smallest → __________________ , __________________ , __________________ ,

__________________ → largest.

A mile is also a unit of length. It is more than 1 km but less than 2 km.

(b) Write the five units of length in order of size, from smallest to largest.

metres	centimetres	miles	kilometres	millimetres

smallest → __________________ , __________________ , __________________ ,

__________________ , __________________ → largest.

4. Match the equivalent lengths.

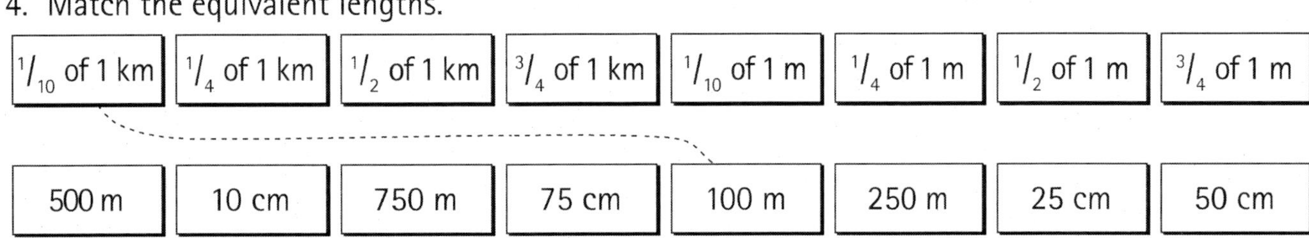

$^1/_{10}$ of 1 km	$^1/_4$ of 1 km	$^1/_2$ of 1 km	$^3/_4$ of 1 km	$^1/_{10}$ of 1 m	$^1/_4$ of 1 m	$^1/_2$ of 1 m	$^3/_4$ of 1 m
500 m	10 cm	750 m	75 cm	100 m	250 m	25 cm	50 cm

5. Convert the centimetres to metres, and vice versa.

(a) 180 cm = _________ m   (b) 237 cm = _________ m   (c) 504 cm = _________ m

(d) 920 cm = _________ m   (e) 1.05 m = _________ cm   (f) 6.59 m = _________ cm

(g) 8.4 m = _________ cm   (h) 0.75 m = _________ cm   (i) 3.5 m = _________ cm

CHALLENGE On the back of the sheet, measure and record the height of five pupils. Write their heights in (a) metres (b) centimetres.

Objectives   • *Knows equivalent units of length.*   • *Converts cm to m and vice versa.*

TESSELLATION

Tessellation is where shapes fit together to form a pattern without any gaps or overlapping.

1. Colour only the shapes that tessellate.

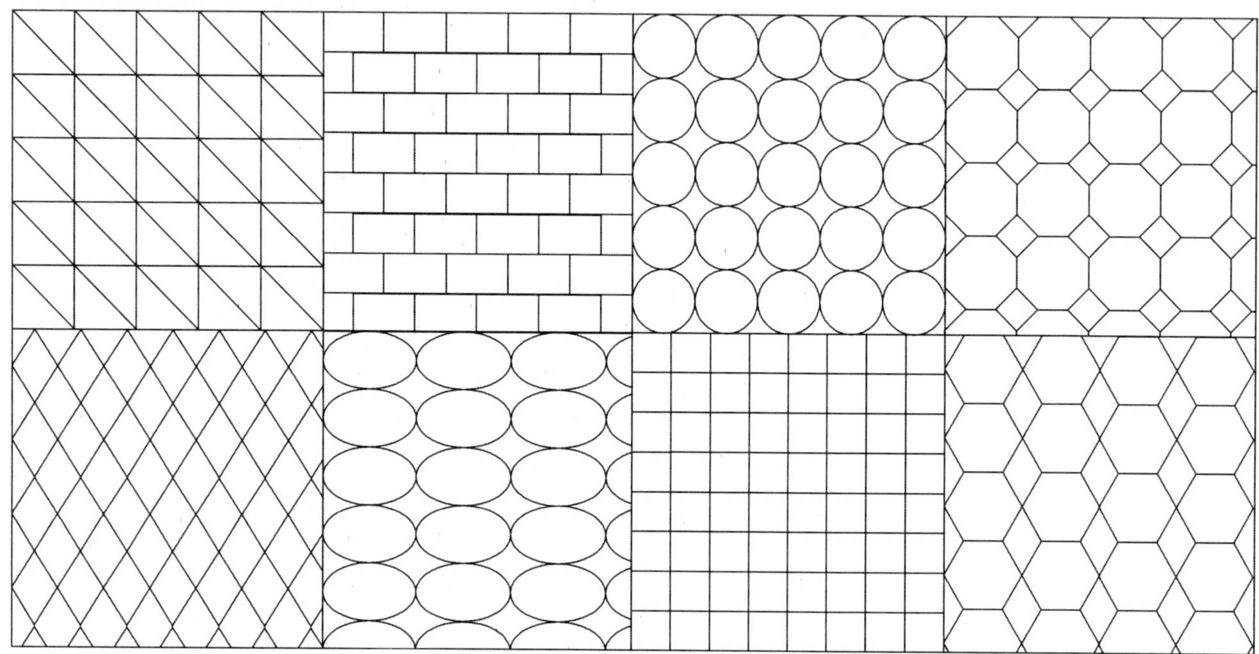

2. Continue these tessellating patterns.

On the back of the sheet, draw your own tessellating pattern and decorate it.

Objective   *Investigates and recognises tessellating shapes.*

TANGRAMS

**A tangram is an Ancient Chinese puzzle, made with seven pieces.
The pieces can be used to make different pictures.**

1. Colour the shapes used in these tangrams.

(a)

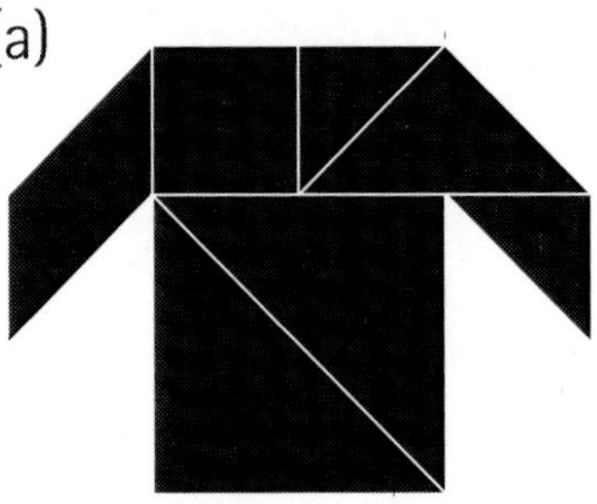

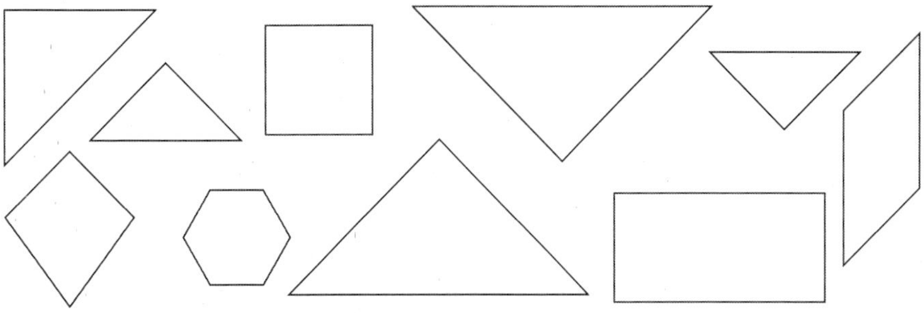

(b)

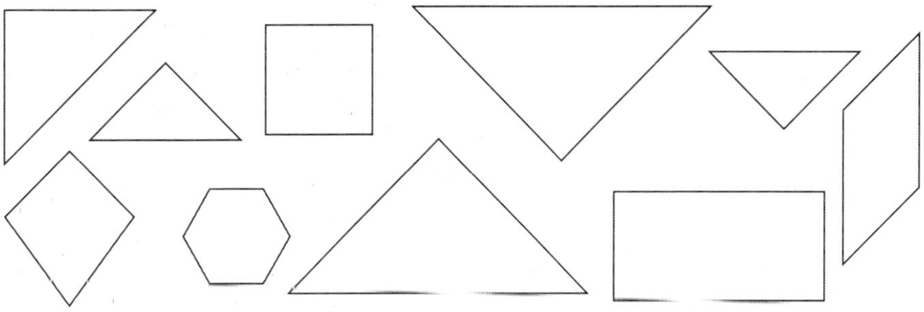

(c)

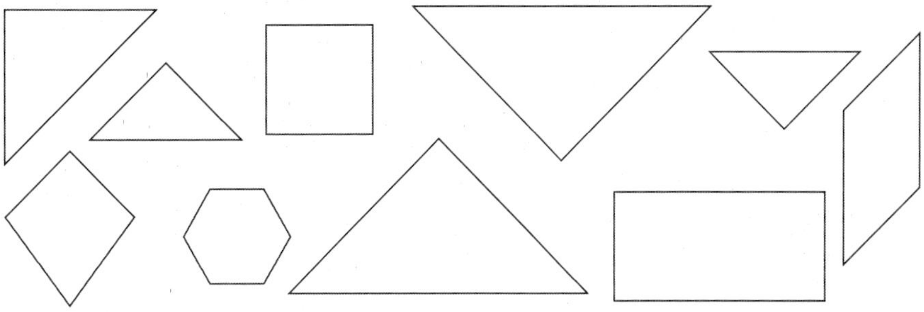

2. Cut out this tangram. Use it to make the pictures above.

CHALLENGE Use the tangram to make your own pictures.

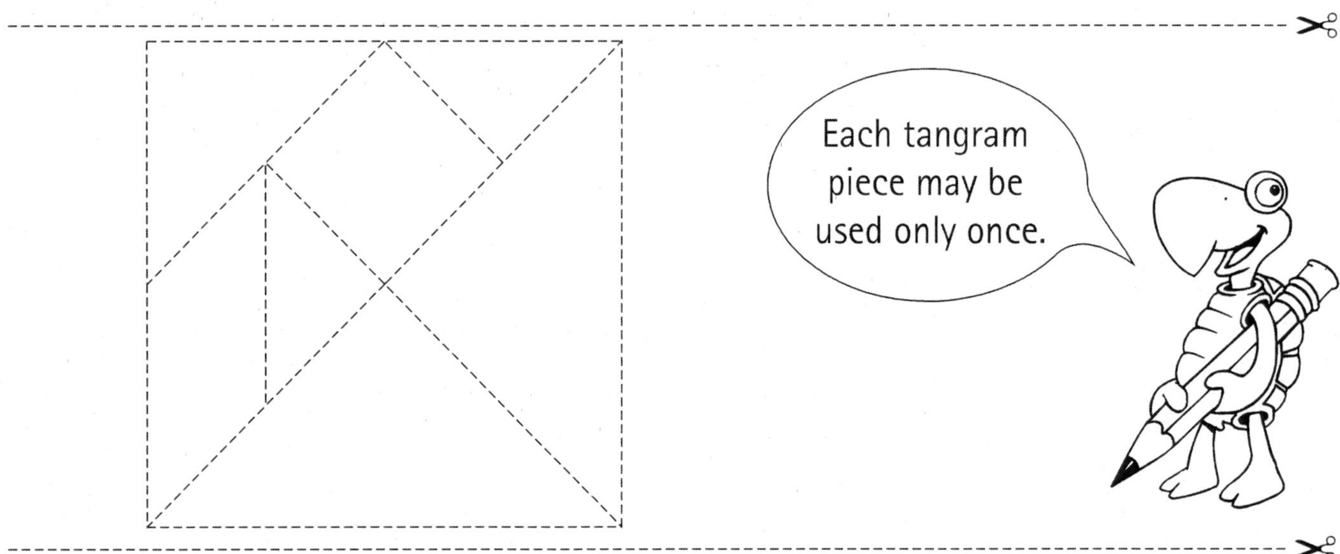

Objective   *Explores the properties of tangrams.*

Magnetic attraction

1 Complete the table. Test each object using a magnet.

Object	Material	Prediction	Attracted?

2 What is similar about the objects attracted to magnets?

3 (a) Do you think a soft drink can will be attracted to a magnet?   yes   no

   (b) Try it. What happens?

Magnetic problems

Problem 1 How can you make a paperclip 'walk' around a paper plate without touching it?

Diagram	What we did

How well did it work?

not good   average   very good

0   1   2   3   4   5

What happened?

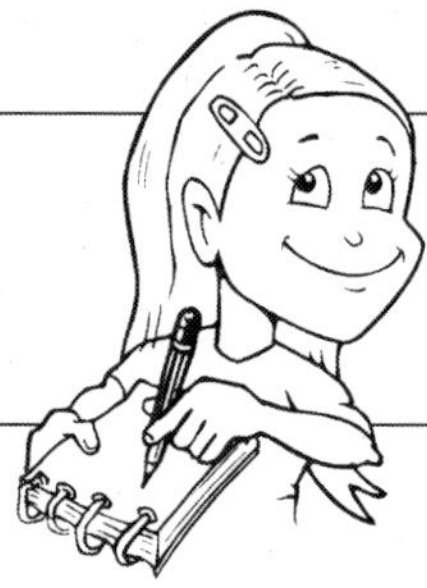

Problem 2 How can you remove a metal object from a narrow jar of water without touching it?

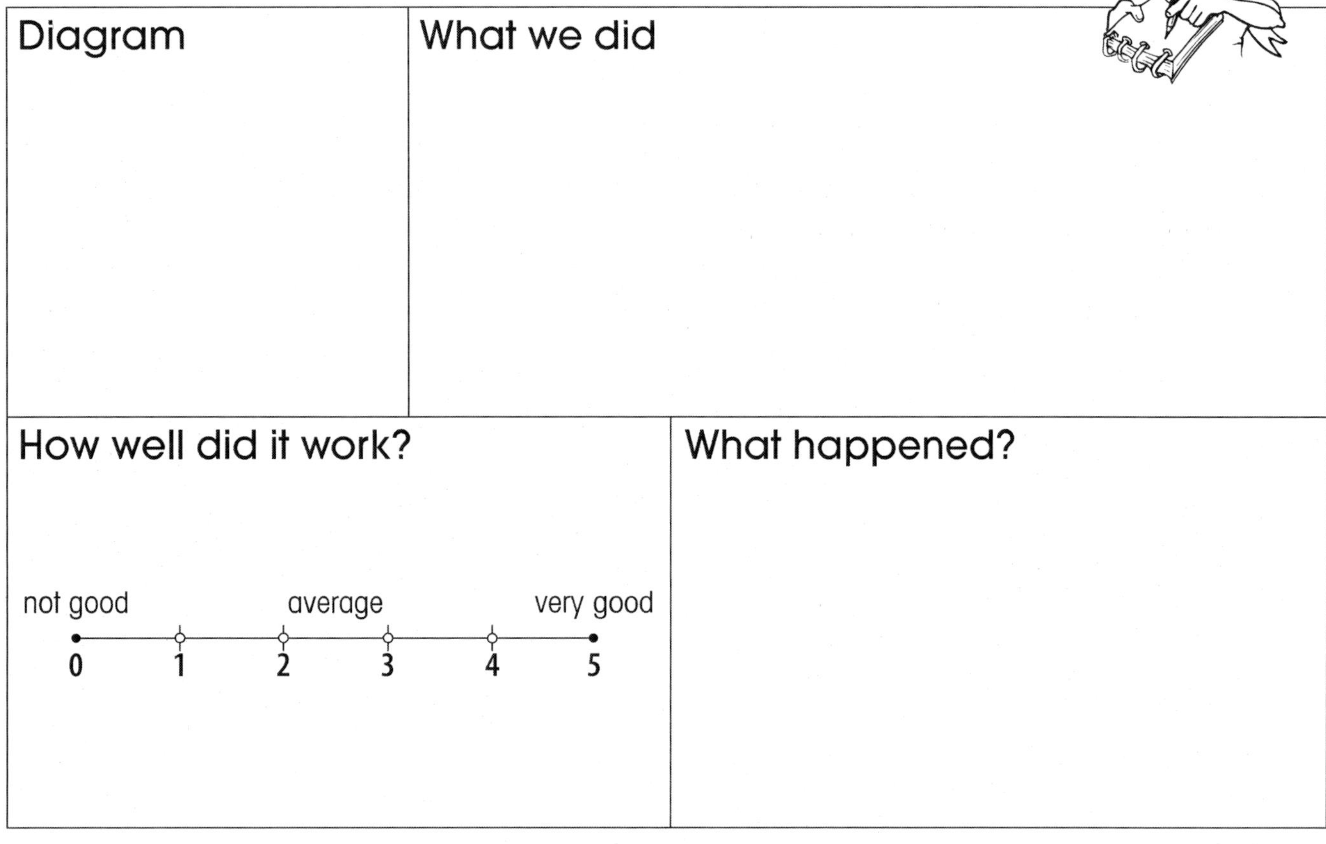

Diagram	What we did

How well did it work?

not good   average   very good

0   1   2   3   4   5

What happened?

Static electricity

1 Try each of the experiments below and record what happens.

(a) A pen is rubbed on a piece of cloth and then brought near a small piece of paper.

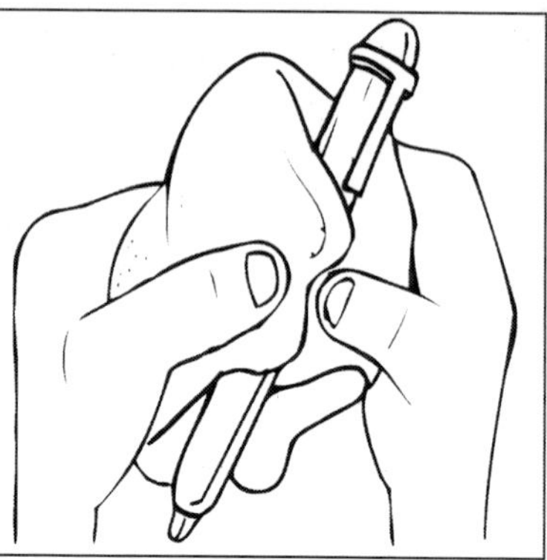

(b) A comb is rubbed on a piece of cloth and then placed near a thin stream of water from a tap.

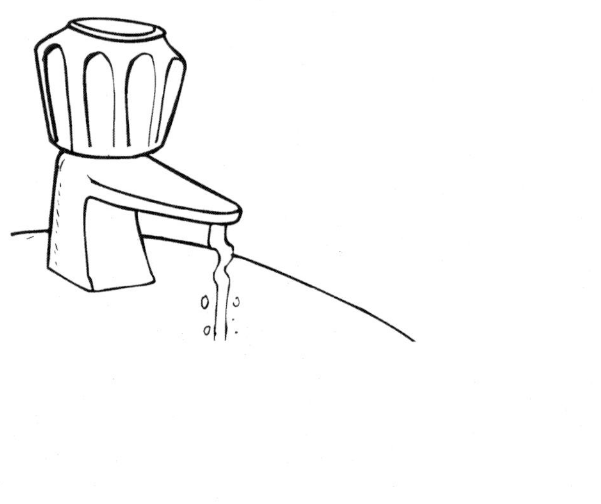

(c) A balloon is rubbed on a woollen jumper and placed near a person's head.

2 Balloon experiment

- When we place two ends of a magnet together, they either join together or they pull apart. Try it!

- Blow up two balloons.

- Tie them to a string and attach them to a door frame with tape. (ask for help!)

- Rub both balloons with wool.

  (a) What happens?
      The balloons …

push together	pull apart

(b) Draw and label what happened.

Electricity

1 Draw and label some electrical appliances you have in your home.

2 (a) How many electric lights do you think there are in your home?

Count them.
How many are there?

(b) How many power points do you think there are in your home?

Count them.
How many are there?

3 Choose the most important item in your home that uses electricity. Draw, label and write about it.

Electricity gives us heat, power and light.

It can also be very dangerous.

4 What do you think this sign means? What should you do if you see it?

WEEK 2

The History of the Olympics – 1

Read this historical timeline.

- *776 BC* — *First recorded Olympic Games; they are held in Olympia in Greece.*

- *330/339 BC* — *Panathenaic Stadium formed between two hills; it is to be used for games.*

- *AD 383* — *Games considered pagan; they are banned by Roman Emperor Theodosius 1.*

- *1850* — *Dr Brookes starts annual games in Shropshire, England; they became known after 1859 as 'the Annual Wenlock Olympic Games'.*

- *1856* — *Wealthy Greek businessman Evangelis Zappas writes to Greek King Otto offering him a donation to fund a revival of the Games every four years. He will also donate prizes for winning athletes.*

- *1859* — *First international Olympic Games held in the city square in Athens, Greece; they are sponsored by Zappas.*

- *1865* — *Death of Zappas. He leaves his fortune to fund the Olympic Games every four years and for the excavation of the Panathenaic Stadium.*

- *1866* — *First Olympic Games held outside Greece, in London but not in a stadium. No Greek athletes competed.*

- *1870* — *First modern international Olympic Games; they are held in a stadium at the Panathenaic Stadium in Athens, with 30 000 spectators attending and funded by Zappas' estate.*

- *1894* — *The International Olympic Committee (IOC) is founded by Baron de Coubertin.*

- *1896* — *First Olympic Games organised by IOC held in Panathenaic Stadium in Athens with athletes from 14 countries competing.*

  First Olympic building, the Zappeion; it is built specifically and used for fencing competitions.

- *1906* — *Second IOC Olympics held in Panathenaic Stadium in Athens with first parade of athletes; the Zappeion used as first athletic village, commemorating its founder.*

- *2004* — *Panathenaic Stadium used for archery and finish of marathon; Zappeion used as the Olympic media Centre.*

- *2012* — *London became the first city to host the Olympics for the third time (it had already hosted them in 1908 and 1948).*

My learning log	When I read this timeline, I could read:	☐ all of it.	☐ most of it.	☐ parts of it.

The History of the Olympics – 2

1. Does the Panathenaic Stadium gives us a clue where this might be located?

2. Why were the Olympic Games banned?

3. Write about how Evangelic Zappas was important to the Olympic Games?

4. What do you think the IOC do?

5. Why do you think the Olympic Games are so popular?

6. What was the Zappeion?

7. Summarise the main events from 1870-1906.

My learning log	While doing these activities:		
	I found Q ______ easy.	I found Q ______ challenging.	I found Q ______ interesting.

The History of the Olympics – 3

1. Use a dictionary to write the meanings of these words.

(a) donation ____

(b) revival ____

(c) sponsored ____

(d) pagan ____

2. Write the root word of each of these words from the text.

(a) considered _______________ (b) offering _______________

(c) excavation _______________ (d) Greek _______________

(e) Roman _______________ (f) revival _______________

3. Match the syllables to make a word.

sta	cher	um
spec	a	thon
ar	ta	y
mar	di	tor

4. Are these words from the text used correctly? Write **Yes** or **No**

(a) The annual games take place three times a year. _______________

(b) The statue commemorates the historic figure. _______________

(c) The mountains are a revival of the power of nature. _______________

(d) The workers had to be excavated because of the fire alarm. _______________

5. Make the past tense of these verbs. (Be careful of some of the spellings.)

(a) record _______________ (b) use _______________

(c) hold _______________ (d) compete _______________

(e) loan _______________ (f) ban _______________

My learning log	*Colour:*	I can / can't make the past tense of some verbs.
		I can / can't use a dictionary to write word definitions.
		I understand / need more practice on root words.

Make Toad-in-the-Hole – 1

Read the recipe for making toad-in-the-hole.

This traditional British dish consists mainly of sausages and batter. Some people think the name comes from the fact that the cooked dish looks like a toad poking its head out of a hole. It is a very old recipe.

Preparation time: 35 minutes   **Cooking time**: 30 minutes   **Serves**: 4–6

Ingredients

- 500 grams good-quality sausages
- 1½ cups plain flour
- 3 eggs, beaten
- 1½ cups milk
- 1 tablespoon melted butter
- 1 tablespoon vegetable oil
- salt and pepper to taste

Equipment and Utensils

- large bowl
- whisk
- casserole dish (approximately 20 x 30 cms or 22 x 22 cms)
- frying pan

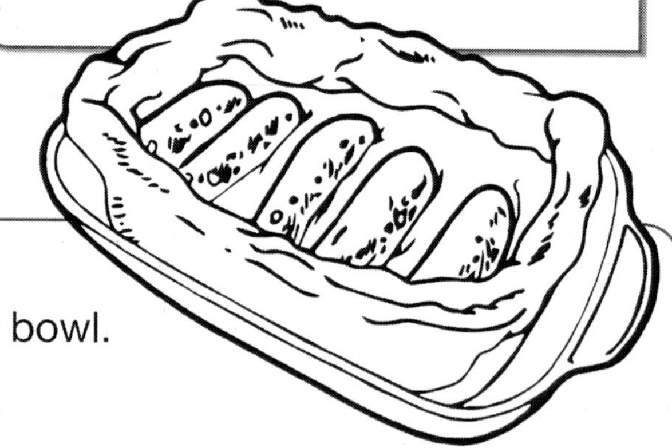

Method

1. Whisk flour, salt and pepper together in bowl.
2. Make a well in centre of seasoned flour.
3. Pour in eggs, milk and butter and whisk until smooth.
4. Cover and stand for 30 minutes.
5. Coat casserole dish with extra vegetable oil.
6. Place empty dish on rack near bottom of oven.
7. Preheat oven to 220° C.
8. Heat tablespoon of oil in frying pan on medium high.
9. Add sausages and brown on at least two sides.
10. Place browned sausages into casserole dish and pour batter over.
11. Cook for about 25–30 minutes until batter is risen and golden.
12. Serve with onion gravy, vegetables and mashed potato.

Test/Evaluation

Do you think this recipe is easy to follow? Do you think the dish will be delicious?

My learning log	When I read this recipe, I could read:	☐ all of it. ☐ most of it. ☐ parts of it.

Make Toad-in-the-Hole – 2

1. Which part of the text gives background information about 'toad-in-the-hole'?

   (a) Ingredients ☐   (b) Equipment and Utensils ☐

   (c) Method ☐   (d) Test/Evaluation ☐

   (e) the first paragraph ☐   (f) the first sentence ☐

2. The purpose of this text is to ____.

3. Do you think the name of this recipe is a suitable one? ⬭ Yes ⬭ No

   Why/Why not? _______________________________________

4. What does 'seasoned flour' mean?

   ____

5. How long will it take to make this recipe from start to finish?

   ____

6. What would happen if you placed the sausages and batter in the dish in the oven without coating it first with oil?

   ____

7. Why is it a good idea to put the items under the headings 'Ingredients' and 'Equipment and Utensils' in a list?

   ____

8. Write the dictionary meanings of the following words.

   (a) sausage _______________________________________

   (b) recipe _______________________________________

   (c) gravy _______________________________________

   (d) equipment _______________________________________

   (e) utensil _______________________________________

9. Why is the word 'approximately' used in regard to the size of the dish?

   ____

My learning log	While doing these activities:		
	I found Q ______ easy.	I found Q ______ challenging.	I found Q ______ interesting.

Make Toad-in-the-Hole – 3

1. Underline the root word and circle the suffix in each word below.

> approximately   beaten   browned   seasoned   mainly

2. Write the root word of each word below.

(a) evaluation _______________

(b) poking _______________

(c) mainly _______________

(d) mashed _______________

(e) preparation _______________

(f) traditional _______________

3. Which word comes from:

(a) the French word 'casse' meaning 'spoon-like container'? _______________

(b) the Latin word meaning 'receive' (instructions)? _______________

(c) the Greek word 'peperi' meaning 'berry'? _______________

4. (a) Write the prefix in the word 'Preheat'. _______________

(b) What do you think the prefix in (a) above means?

____

5. Find and write words in the text with the following suffixes.

(a) –ous

(b) –ly

(c) –ion

6. Write homophones from the text for the words below.

(a) reed _______________

(b) whole _______________

(c) sum _______________

(d) plane _______________

(e) flower _______________

(f) paw _______________

7. Command verbs are used to give instructions. Twelve are used in the 'Method' part of the recipe. Write them below.

My learning log	Colour:	I can / can't recognise root words.
		I understand / need more practice on suffixes.
		I can / can't recognise command verbs.

Verbs

A **verb** is a word which shows actions, or states of being or having. Being verbs include *am*, *is*, *are*, *was* and *were*. Having verbs include *has*, *had* and *have*.

1. (a) Read the report below.

    *Mongooses **are** carnivorous mammals. Usually, they **are found** in South Asia and Africa. Mongooses **hunt** small animals, eggs and, sometimes, fruit for food. They **live** in rocky crevices and holes and often **dig** burrows. They **have** long bodies with rough, shaggy hair, pointed noses and long, bushy tails. Some mongooses **kill** snakes, including cobras. They quickly **dodge** the snake each time it **strikes** until the snake **tires**. Mongooses then **seize** the snake's head in their jaws, **crush** its skull and **eat** it. The dead snake's venom **is** harmless to the mongoose.*

    (b) Choose two different coloured pencils or markers. Use one to identify all the 'being' verbs and the other to identify all the 'having' verbs.

    (c) Write all the verbs which show action in the box below.

2. Write a list of about 10 action verbs to use in a text about snakes.

3. Complete the table.

Snakes are ...	Snakes have ...

4. Use the action verbs in Question 2 and the information above to write a short report about snakes on a separate sheet of paper.

Command verbs

> **Command verbs** are verbs used to order, command or give instructions. They can usually be found at the beginning of a sentence in a procedure.

1. (a) Read the procedure.

Fake blood

Ingredients and equipment

- *250 mL smooth peanut butter*
- *125 mL non-sudsy soap powder*
- *30 mL red food colouring*
- *1 L white corn syrup*
- *about 15 drops blue food colouring*
- *bowl, spoon, airtight container*

Method

1. *Mix peanut butter with small amount of corn syrup in bowl to make a runny mixture.*
2. *Add soap and food colourings.*
3. *Stir well.*
4. *Add more corn syrup until of desired consistency.*
5. *Refrigerate any unused 'blood' in an airtight container.*

(b) Write the five command verbs used in the procedure.

____

____

2. Use the command verbs below to complete the sentences.

Hand	*Step*	*Hold*	*slide*	*Put*	*Brush*	*tie*

(a) _____________________ tightly to the string of the kite!

(b) _____________________ to the left and _____________________ to the right. That's the next part of the dance.

(c) _____________________ your hair and _____________________ it back with a band.

(d) _____________________ your homework in now, please!

(e) _____________________ the bottles in the recycling bin.

3. Think of something that requires simple instructions to explain to a friend; for example, how to shade a picture, fanfold a sheet of paper, sketch a face, work out fractions or address an envelope. Ask your friend to write down your oral instructions, then, together, highlight the command verbs.

Whistlestop tour

Dear Grandma Alice

I must tell you about the wonderful capital cities tour we did as part of our August holiday in Europe. Mum, Dad and I had the best time! We didn't stay in any hotels because, after dinner each night, we took a train to the next city, arriving there early the following morning.

Day 1: Amsterdam, Netherlands. Our first stop was Anne Frank's house where she wrote her diary while she and her family were hiding from the Germans. It was so sad. Mum and I both cried. Dad was very quiet too. After lunch, we visited the Van Gogh museum. Did you know he was Amsterdam's most famous artist? Later on, we went to the Bloemenmarkt, a world famous floating flower market. The flowers were stunning but we didn't think it was a good idea to buy any!

Day 2: Brussels, Belgium. In the morning, we strolled through the Grand Place, a 13th century market. I loved the medieval Town Hall with its crooked spire, topped with a statue of archangel St Michael slaying the devil! At midday, we joined a tour around the Royal Palace before enjoying a relaxing picnic lunch in Brussels Park. Dad and I both fell asleep while Mum read her book. Our last visit of the day was to Mini Europe, which has 300 doll-sized versions of Europe's most famous monuments. It was so cool!

Day 3: Paris, France. In the morning, we climbed the Eiffel Tower. The view of the city was amazing! Later on, we took a boat trip on the River Seine, followed by a drive along the famous Champs Elysee, and then passed the Arc de Triomphe, where the Tour de France finishes each year. We ended the day by attending a service at the Sacré-Coeur Church.

Day 4: Vienna, Austria. Our last day! In the morning, we wandered around Marie Antoinette's childhood home, the Schonbrunn Palace. It's quite magnificent. We lazed in the gardens for a while before going to the Spanish Riding School to see the Lipizzaner horses practising their dressage. Then after dinner, it was off to the airport!

Well, Grandma, we're back home now and I'm busy with my diary and photographs because I'm writing a book about my holiday. I've collected lots of maps and leaflets from the places we visited. I've never enjoyed a holiday so much! When I grow up, I want to travel the world!

With love from Sally

Use the recount on page 15 to complete the page.

1. Title

(a) Do you think the title tells you about the content of the letter?

yes no

(b) If you answered yes, explain why. If you answered no, suggest two alternative titles.

2. Orientation

Match the answers to the questions.

(a) What? •   • Dad, Mum, Sally

(b) Where? •   • By train

(c) Who? •   • Capital cities tour

(d) How? •   • Europe

3. Events

(a) Label the attractions in the order they were visited. Start with number one.

(i) Mini Europe ☐

(ii) Schonbrunn Palace ☐

(iii) Bloemenmarkt ☐

(iv) Sacré-Coeur Church ☐

(v) Eiffel Tower ☐

(vi) Van Gogh museum ☐

(b) Write three words or phrases from the text that suggest the passing of time.

4. Conclusion

What information does the conclusion give us about how much Sally enjoyed her holiday?

1. Plan a recount in the form of a letter to a friend about your holiday.

Title

Orientation

Events

Conclusion

2. Write your recount.

3. Edit your work.

Using a washing machine

Read the procedure.

requirements:

- water
- washing machine
- electricity supply
- items (to/too/two) be washed
- detergent

method:

- (separate/seperate) light and dark coloured items
- place a load in machine without overloading
- add correct amount (of/off) detergent
- close machine
- set load size
- choose correct water temperature
- select washing programme
- check water is turned on
- insert machine plug into socket
- turn on electricity supply
- start machine

evaluation:

- was (your/yore) washing clean

Editing skills

❶ *Punctuation*

(a) The procedure needs 15 capital letters, 11 full stops and 1 question mark. Circle 3 colons.

❷ *Spelling*

(a) Circle the correct word in each bracket.

❸ *Grammar*

A command verb tells us what to do.

(a) Underline all the command verbs in the text.

(b) How many are there? _________

Some words can be either verbs or nouns depending on their meaning within the sentence; for example:

Walk to the door. (verb)

We enjoyed our walk. (noun)

(c) Circle the words below that could be used as either a noun or a verb.

play   sleep   drink   open

(d) Choose one word and use it to write two sentences. Use it as a noun in one sentence and as a verb in the other.

- _______________________________

____

- _______________________________

____

❹ *Vocabulary*

Compound words are two words joined together as one.

(a) There are 2 compound words in the text. Find and circle each.

My Siamese cat

Read the description.

when i went to look at a (litter/litta) of five kittens, they all looked so cute that i cuddled them all one (keeped/kept) coming back to me the owners said that he had obviously chosen me and that he (wos/was) the (one/won) i should (by/buy), so i did

his full name is kwanlee cheong hoi, but we call him cheong he is (wite/white) with chocolate-brown ears face and (tale/tail) and (bright/brite) blue eyes like all siamese cats, he is sleek and elegant and he walks in a (prowd/proud) and aloof (manner/manna)

cheong chose me and he makes it very clear that he is in charge he has trained me well, issuing his orders for food or attention in a very (loud/lowd) voice which is hard to ignore, especially (wen/when) i am speaking on the (telephone/telaphone)

when mum picks up her keys, he races to the car and stretches out along the back window ledge (ready/reddy) to (injoy/enjoy) the drive

cheong is a wonderful pet and an important part of my life

❶ Punctuation

(a) The description needs 10 capital letters to start sentences, 10 full stops, 6 capital letters for proper nouns, 5 for the word 'I' and 1 comma in a list in paragraph 2.

❷ Spelling

(a) Circle the correct word in each bracket.

❸ Grammar

Pronouns are words used instead of nouns; for example, 'I', 'he', 'they'.

(a) Underline an example of a pronoun in each paragraph.

(b) Match the pronouns. One has been done for you.

he	hers
she	ours
we	his
they	its
it	theirs

Adjectives are used to describe nouns.

(c) List 4 of the adjectives used to describe the cat in the text.

______________   ______________

______________   ______________

(d) Write 6 other adjectives you would use to describe a cat.

______________   ______________

______________   ______________

______________   ______________

❹ Writing

(a) Which paragraph describes Cheong's physical features? ______

Wonderwings

imagine soaring high in the sky, experiencing the thrill of flite ...

have you ever wished you had the abilitee to fly like a bird To just flap your arms and take off into the open sky? well, with WONDERWINGS, now you can!

aerodynamically designed non-polluting, fully tested WONDERWINGS can help you take to the skies simply strap them onto your back, and you're up up and away! so simple, anyone can try it it's easy

100% fether-lined WONDERWINGS sold out in other contries within days of being advertised—don't miss out

with WONDERWINGS you can saw like an egle order your pair today!

❶ Punctuation

(a) The advert needs 9 capital letters used for beginning sentences, 3 full stops, 2 exclamation marks and 1 question mark.

(b) Two commas are missing in paragraph 3 and one comma in paragraph 5.

❷ Spelling

(a) Six words are misspelt. Write the correct spelling.

_______________ _______________

_______________ _______________

_______________ _______________

❸ Grammar

(a) Write the words in the text that follow 'a' and 'an'.

a _________________________

an _________________________

(b) Write 'a' or 'an' in front of these words.

(i) _____ penguin   (ii) _____ owl

(iii) _____ ant   (iv) _____ kitten

❹ Vocabulary

Similes compare one thing to another; for example, 'like a bird', 'like an eagle' and 'as cold as ice'.

(a) Write a simile to complete these sentences.

(i) The baby's skin is as

____

(ii) My dog acts like

____

(iii) The wind felt as

____

(iv) The lake looks like

____

MORE MULTIPLES

1. Fill in the missing numbers and write the rule.

skip counting pattern	pattern rule
(a) 0, _______, 2000, 3000, _______, _______	
(b) 150, _______, 100, 75, _______, _______, 0	
(c) 6, _______, _______, 24, 30, _______, 42, _______	
(d) 90, 81, _______, _______, _______, 45, _______, 27	
(e) 21, _______, 35, 42, _______, 56, _______, _______	

2. Complete the skip counting patterns.

(a) Forwards in 9s from 18. 18, _______, _______, _______, _______, _______.

(b) Forwards in 7s from 21. 21, _______, _______, _______, _______, _______.

(c) Forwards in 6s from 12. 12, _______, _______, _______, _______, _______.

(d) Forwards in 25s from 100. 100, _______, _______, _______, _______, _______.

(e) Backwards in 1000s from 8000. 8000, _______, _______, _______,

_______, _______.

(f) Backwards in 9s from 108. 108, _______, _______, _______, _______, _______.

(g) Backwards in 7s from 84. 84, _______, _______, _______, _______, _______.

CHALLENGE

On the back of the sheet, skip count from 606 to 660 in 6s.

Objective   *Counts forwards and backwards.*

1000 MORE OR LESS

1. Complete the chart.

	1000 more	1000 less		1000 more	1000 less
(a) 3651			(g) 1569		
(b) 5250			(h) 6360		
(c) 8463			(i) 9547		
(d) 4024			(j) 2880		
(e) 2981			(k) 1090		
(f) 7509			(l) 9543		

2. Count forwards or backwards in 1000s from the following numbers.

(a) forwards   567, _______, _______, _______, _______, _______.

(b) forwards   8924, _______, _______, _______, _______, _______.

(c) forwards   6320, _______, _______, _______, _______, _______.

(d) forwards   9663, _______, _______, _______, _______, _______.

(e) backwards   8421, _______, _______, _______, _______, _______.

(f) backwards   6057, _______, _______, _______, _______, _______.

(g) backwards   15 212, _______, _______, _______, _______, _______.

(h) backwards   12 604, _______, _______, _______, _______, _______.

3. Draw lines to match with the number that is 1000 more.

265	9265	10 265	19 265	24 265	29 265

11 265	25 265	1265	30 265	10 265	20 265

4. Draw lines to match with the number that is 1000 less.

1021	1621	2021	15 021	20 021	29 021

1921	19 021	21	28 021	14 021	621

CHALLENGE

Count backwards in 10 000s.

150 000, _______, 130 000, 120 000, _______, _______, 90 000,

_______, _______, 60 000, _______, 40 000, _______, 20 000, _______, 0.

ADDING WITH TRADING

When adding with two or more digits, if two numbers add to more than 10, we need to trade the 10 ones for 1 ten and write it in the tens column. Look at the example below.

9 + 5 = 14, so the 10 from the number 14 is traded into the tens column and added with the tens.

6 + 5 + 1 (traded 10) = 12 tens, so the 100 from 120 is traded to the hundreds column.

hundreds	tens	ones
	6	9
+	5	5
1	②2	①4

69 + 55 = 124

1. Add these two-digit numbers and remember to trade.

(a)   3 8
      + 1 3
      ______

(b)   2 9
      + 1 5
      ______

(c)   4 5
      + 2 7
      ______

(d)   3 8
      + 3 4
      ______

(e)   3 2 9
    + 4 2 8
    ____

(f)   2 5 2
    + 1 3 9
    ____

(g)   5 4 8
    + 3 3 6
    ____

(h)   6 5 5
    + 3 2 8
    ____

(i)   1 5 9
    + 8 3 4
    ____

(j)   5 3 7
    + 2 3 9
    ____

(k)   1 5 9
    + 4 4 6
    ____

(l)   2 8 5
    + 3 4 5
    ____

(m)   6 8 7
    + 2 1 3
    ____

(n)   5 4 9
    + 2 5 6
    ____

(o)   3 7 2
    + 4 8 9
    ____

(p)   2 6 8
    + 6 8 6
    ____

2. In your own words, describe how you solved 1(n).

____

____

CHALLENGE

On the back of the sheet, set these addition sums out vertically and solve them.

(a) 75 + 39   (b) 58 + 39   (c) 482 + 239   (d) 567 + 365

Objective   *Uses knowledge of place value to solve addition problems with two digits.*

SUBTRACTING WITH TRADING

When subtracting with two or more digits, if the top number is smaller than the bottom number, we need to trade a ten from the tens column and write it in the ones column. Look at the example below.

73 – 36 = ?, start with the ones. Ten is traded from the tens column to become 13 – 6 = 7.

The tens column has now become 6 – 3 = 3

	tens	ones
	⨉ 6 →	①3
–	3	6
	3	7

73 – 36 = 37

1. Subtract these two-digit numbers. Remember to trade.

(a)	3 4 – 1 6	(b)	2 2 – 1 5	(c)	4 3 – 1 7	(d)	4 5 – 2 8

(e)	8 5 3 – 4 2 5	(f)	9 7 2 – 2 3 9	(g)	8 5 6 – 1 2 8	(h)	5 6 5 – 2 3 9

(i)	7 9 4 – 3 4 9	(j)	5 8 3 – 3 2 7	(k)	8 7 0 – 7 5 1	(l)	9 9 3 – 8 6 6

(m)	5 5 0 – 2 9	(n)	7 4 1 – 4 3 8	(o)	3 8 5 – 2 5 8	(p)	9 7 5 – 8 5 7

2. In your own words, describe how you solved 1(o).

____

____

CHALLENGE

Check your answers. Tick (✔) them if they are correct and cross (✗) them if they are incorrect. Rework any incorrect solutions.

Objective   *Uses knowledge of place value to solve subtraction problems with two and three digits.*

LENGTH PROBLEMS

1. Convert the metres to kilometres.

   (a) 1000 m = ____1____ km   (b) 1250 m = _________ km   (c) 2500 m = _________ km

   (d) 2750 m = _________ km   (e) 4600 m = _________ km   (f) 5840 m = _________ km

   (g) 7200 m = _________ km   (h) 12 380 m = _________ km   (i) 15 899 m = _________ km

2. Decide whether you will add, subtract, multiply or divide to answer these word problems. Then solve them.

Word problem	+ / − / x / ÷	Working out	Answer
(a) Three snakes are 70 cm, 65 cm and 95 cm long. What is their total length in metres?	+ − x ÷		
(b) A rope is 2.55 m in length. Raiza cuts off 75 cm. Sam cuts off another 55 cm. How long is the rope in centimetres?	+ − x ÷		
(c) Ribbon is bought in lengths of 1.25 m. Sam buys five lengths. How long is the ribbon Sam has bought in centimetres?	+ − x ÷		
(d) Jack sets off to drive 366 km from Bristol to Glasgow. When he reaches Manchester he has driven 161 km. How many more kilometres is it to Glasgow?	+ − x ÷		
(e) Each side of a square field is 1.25 km. What is the perimeter of the field in metres?	+ − x ÷		

CHALLENGE Write a word problem to match the sum 15 cm + 17 cm + 24 cm = 56 cm.

Objective   *Converts between different units of measurement.*

EQUIVALENT MASSES AND CAPACITIES

1. Match the units of measure to the correct abbreviation.

(a) grams •		• kg
(b) kilograms •		• mL
(c) millilitres •		• L
(d) litres •		• g

2. Answer these statements.

(a) There are __________ grams in 1 kilogram.   (b) There are __________ millilitres in 1 litre.

3. **A pint is another measure of capacity. It is roughly equal to half a litre.**

Write the three units of capacity in order of size, from smallest to largest.

pint   litre   millilitre

smallest → __________________ , __________________ , __________________ → largest.

4. Match the equivalent measurements.

$^1/_{10}$ of 1 kg	$^1/_4$ of 1 kg	$^1/_2$ of 1 kg	$^3/_4$ of 1 kg	$^1/_{10}$ of 1 L	$^1/_4$ of 1 L	$^1/_2$ of 1 L	$^3/_4$ of 1 L

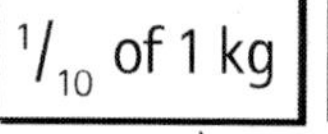

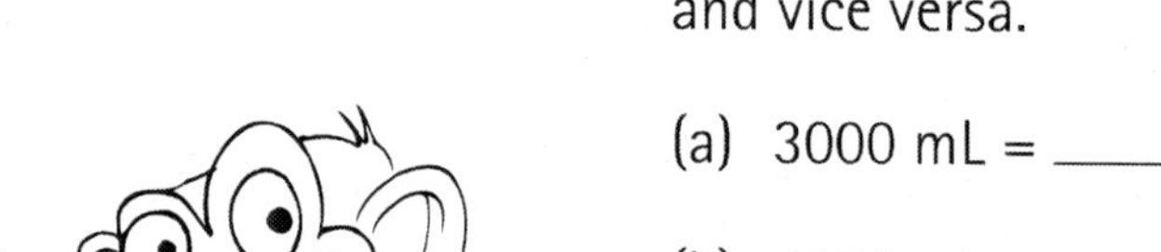
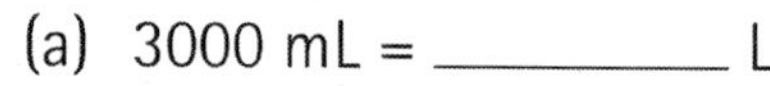

500 g	250 mL	750 g	100 mL	100 g	750 mL	250 g	500 mL

5. Convert the grams to kilograms, and vice versa.

(a) 4000 g = __________ kg

(b) 7500 g = __________ kg

(c) 8750 g = __________ kg

(d) 2.5 kg = __________ g

(e) 5.8 kg = __________ g

(f) 6.1 kg = __________ g

(g) 7.4 kg = __________ g

6. Convert the millilitres to litres, and vice versa.

(a) 3000 mL = __________ L

(b) 4250 mL = __________ L

(c) 9500 mL = __________ L

(d) 6.7 L = __________ mL

(e) 7.5 L = __________ mL

(f) 4.2 L = __________ mL

(g) 6.6 L = __________ mL

CHALLENGE

On the back of the sheet, weigh and record the mass of five books.
Write the mass in (a) kilograms (b) grams.

Objectives   • *Knows equivalent units of mass and capacity.*   • *Converts kg to g and L to mL, and vice versa.*

2-D SHAPES

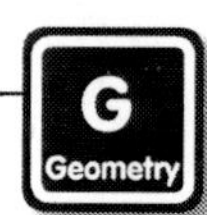

1. Write the name of each shape.

circle, square, triangle, rectangle, pentagon, hexagon, heptagon, octagon

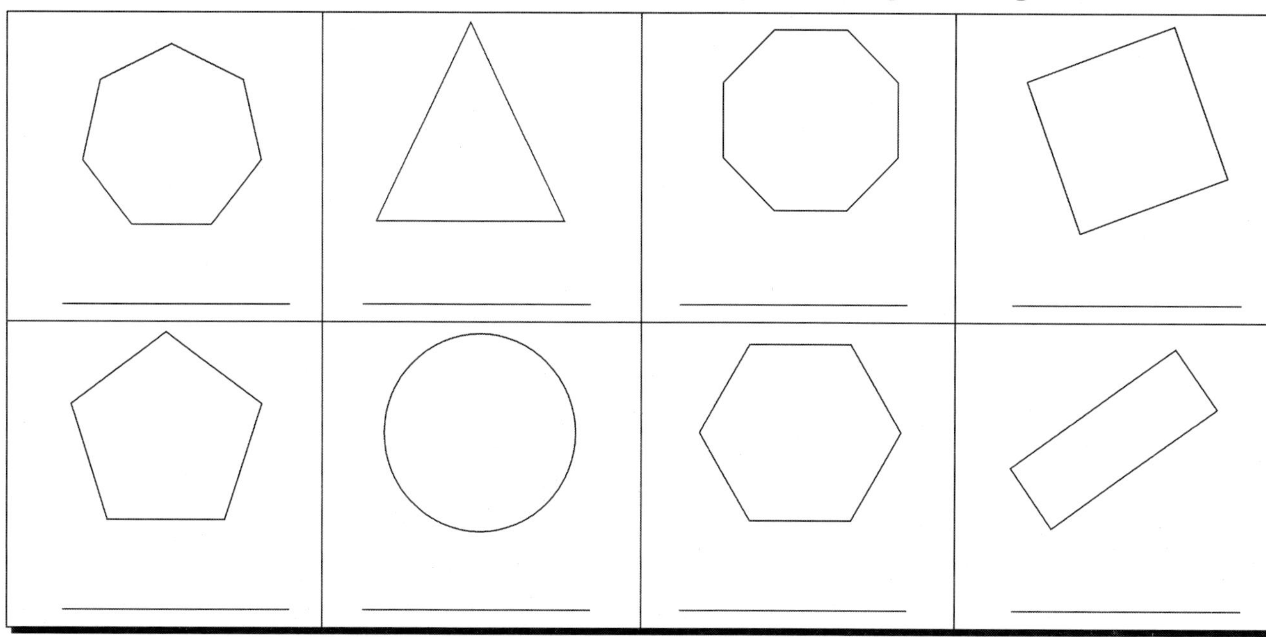

2. Polygons are shapes that are made up of three or more straight sides. Colour in the polygons.

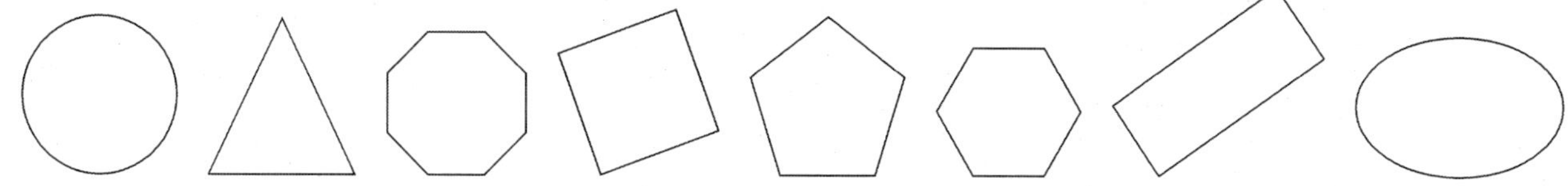

3. Triangles are shapes that are made up of three straight sides.
   Match each triangle to its name and description.

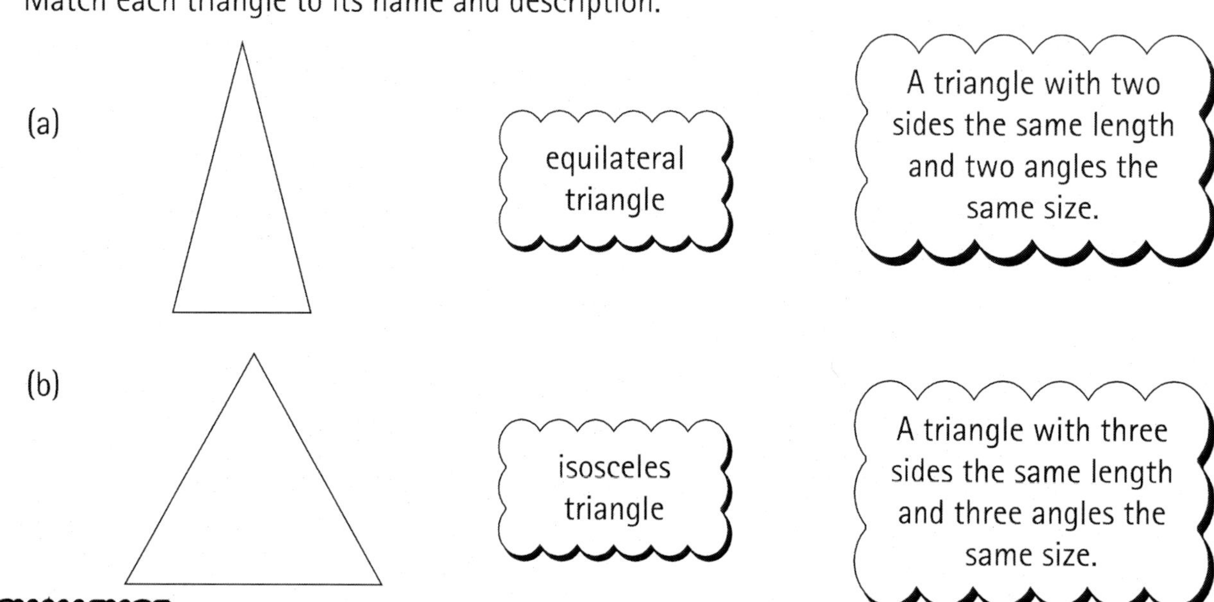

CHALLENGE

On the back of the sheet, draw three different polygons using a ruler and name them.

Objective	*Recognises, compares and names 2-D shapes.*

DESCRIBING 2-D SHAPES

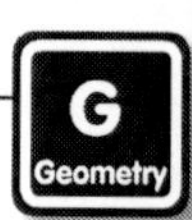

1. Look at the shape, then fill in the description and shape name.

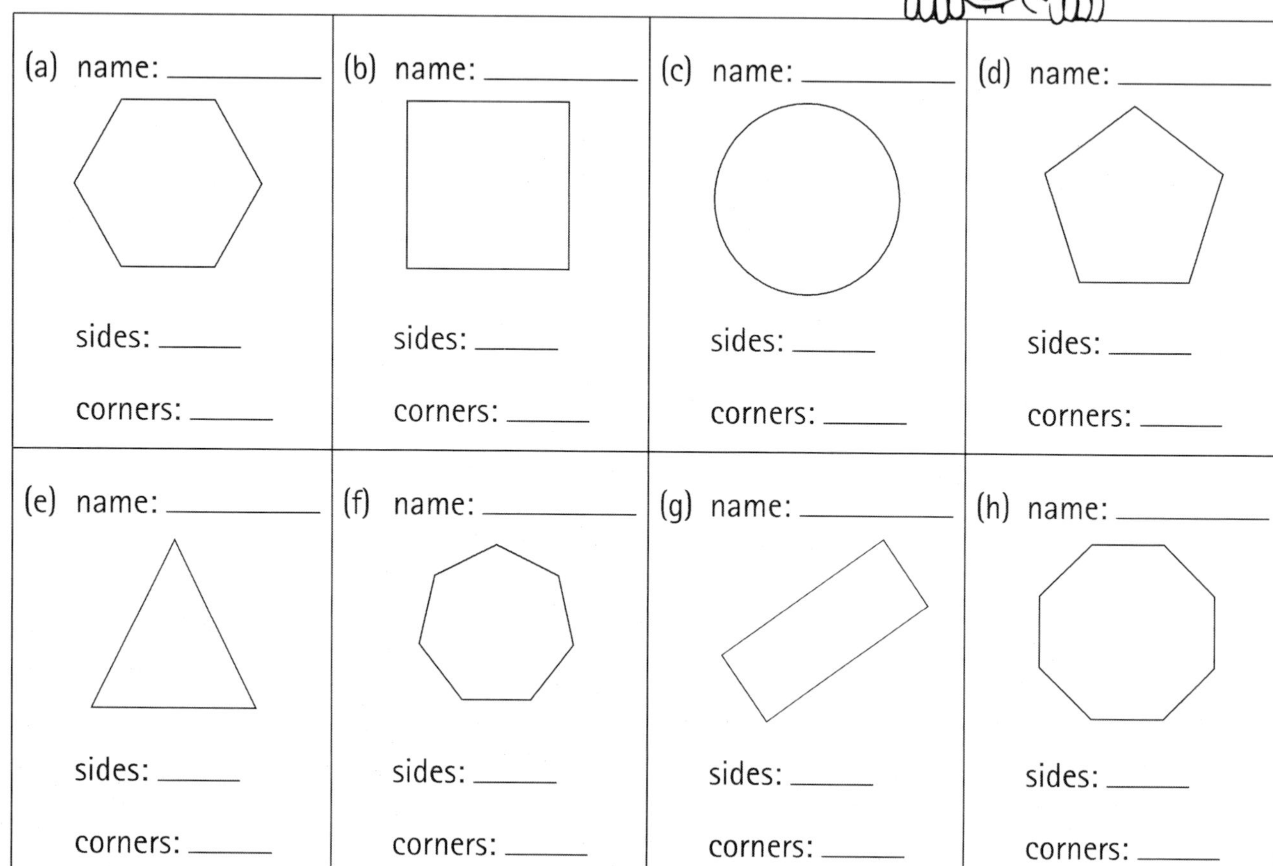

(a) name: ___________ sides: _____ corners: _____	(b) name: ___________ sides: _____ corners: _____

(a) name: ___________ sides: _____ corners: _____
(b) name: ___________ sides: _____ corners: _____
(c) name: ___________ sides: _____ corners: _____
(d) name: ___________ sides: _____ corners: _____
(e) name: ___________ sides: _____ corners: _____
(f) name: ___________ sides: _____ corners: _____
(g) name: ___________ sides: _____ corners: _____
(h) name: ___________ sides: _____ corners: _____

2. Read the description and name and draw the shape.

(a) a three-sided polygon with three angles the same size	(b) a quadrilateral with four equal sides and four right angles	(c) a polygon with seven equal sides
(d) a three-sided polygon with two sides the same length and one line of symmetry	(e) a polygon with five equal sides and five corners	(f) a quadrilateral with two short and two long sides and four right angles

CHALLENGE

On the back of the sheet, make a list of all the different triangles you can see in the classroom.

Objective   *Recognises, draws and describes 2-D shapes using simple spatial language.*

Push or pull?

1 Add more objects to the list. Write or draw them.

Needs a push to move	Needs a pull to move	Needs a push or pull
wheelbarrow	kite	shopping trolley

2 Design a 'yacht' that can **move on land by wind**. Your vehicle is going to be used to carry toys.

3 Draw the 'yacht' you made. Label each part.

4 How did your yacht move?

5 How could you improve it?

Down the ramp!

1 Test each object below to see if it will roll or slide down a ramp.
Make a guess before you start. Add two more of your own.

Object	Guess	Rolls	Slides	Neither

2 (a) Which object rolled the fastest? _______________________________

(b) Which object slid the fastest? _______________________________

3 Choose an object that did not roll or slide. _______________________

Explain why. ____

____

4 Circle which ramp would make a marble roll further.

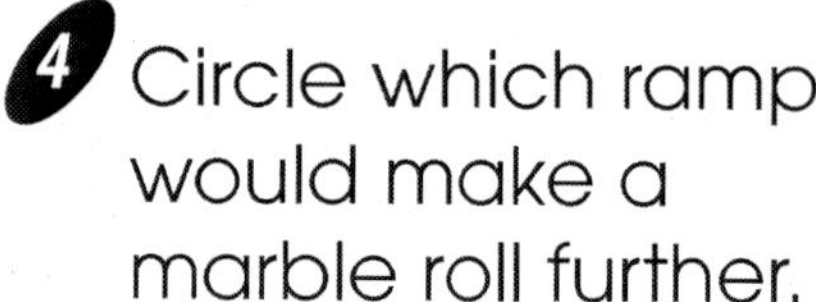
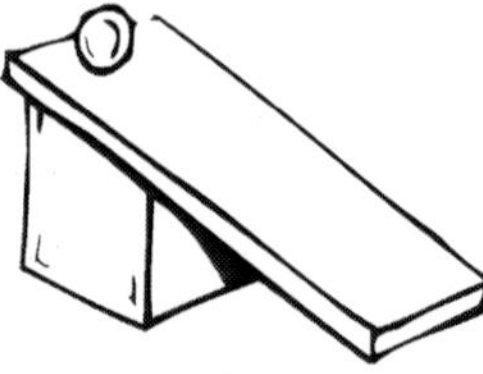
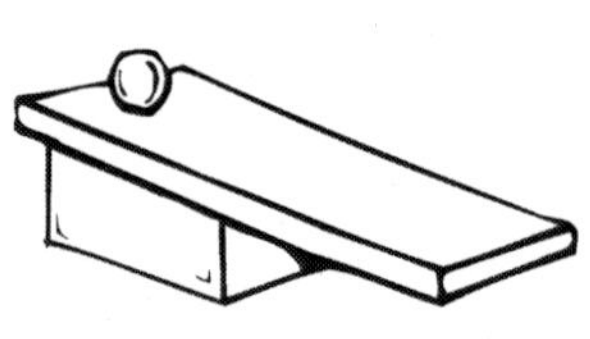

Float or sink?

1 Draw five objects you are going to test. Complete the table.

Object	Material	Prediction	Float or sink?

2 Record what you found out about objects that float or sink.

____

____

Some objects that sink can be made to float if they are hollowed out.

3 Use modelling clay to see if this is true. Draw and write about what you discovered.

WEEK 3

ENGLISH

MATHEMATICS

SCIENCE

Mr Miacca – 1

Read this version of the folk tale.

Tommy Grimes was sometimes a good boy and often a bad boy; and he could be a very bad boy! Tommy's mother was always saying to him, 'Dear Tommy, be a good boy and listen to your wise old mother. Don't go out of our street, for if you do Mr Miacca will take you home to eat for his supper.' But because Tommy was, at times, a very bad boy, he of course didn't listen to his mother's wise words of warning. One day he'd scarcely turned the corner out of his street when the huge and frightening Mr Miacca snapped him up, dropped him head first into a sack, hoisted him over his shoulder and took him home.

In his house, Mr Miacca pulled Tommy out of the sack and pinched at his arms and legs. 'You're quite tough compared to the others', he commented, 'but you're all there is for supper and you'll 'ave to do!' After a pause, a bothered looking Mr Miacca exclaimed, 'Blimey! I've forgot the 'erbs and it's rubbish you'll taste without the 'erbs. Sally, come in 'ere to me ... SALLY!' He called out to his wife.

Mrs Miacca soon appeared saying, 'What is it you want dear 'usband?'

'Look 'ere Sally, 'ere's a tough little boy for our supper', said Mr Miacca, 'but I've forgot the 'erbs, so watch 'im while I go fetch 'em will ya?'

'Right you are then, so I will', Mrs Miacca answered as Mr Miacca went off.

Clever Tommy began talking to Mrs Miacca. He asked if they always ate little boys and she explained they usually did. 'What about some pudding?' Tommy asked. 'You must get tired of boy meat all the time?' Mrs Miacca's face lit up and Tommy went on. 'My mother is making a pudding this very day. I'm sure she'd give you some if I ask her. Shall I run and get you some now?'

'Ah what a thoughtful boy you are. Go on now and be sure to be back before Mr Miacca won't you', Mrs Miacca answered.

Tommy ran home, as relieved as a boy could be to have escaped the pot! He was a good boy for many weeks after, but of course that didn't last. Once again Tommy left the street and once again he was quickly snapped up into Mr Miacca's sack.

This time Mr Miacca wasn't taking any chances. He put Tommy under the sofa and sat on it while the pot boiled. Tired of waiting, Mr Miacca ordered, 'Put your leg out now and I'll chop it off to throw in the pot. That'll stop you running off again!' Tommy put out a leg and it was promptly chopped off and added to the pot.

Mr Miacca went to find Sally in the other room and Tommy crept out from under the sofa and bolted home! It was the sofa leg he had put out and not his own!

My learning log	When I read this folk tale, I could read:	all of it.	most of it.	parts of it.

Mr Miacca – 2

1. This folk tale is being told to:

   (a) make people laugh. ☐

   (b) explain a natural feature. ☐

   (c) warn children of danger. ☐

2. Explain some of the features of Mr and Mrs Miacca's speech. Is it formal or informal?

   ____

   ____

3. Why has the author dropped the letter 'h' from the speech in the text?

   ____

4. Write some adjectives to describe each character from the story.

   (a) Tommy Grimes: ____

   (b) Mr Miacca: ____

   (c) Mrs Miacca: ____

5. Explain how you think each character felt and acted.

   (a) Tommy's mother when he went missing.

   ____

   ____

   (b) Mrs Miacca when Tommy didn't return with the pudding.

   ____

   ____

   (c) Mr Miacca when he realised that Tommy had escaped.

   ____

   ____

My learning log	While doing these activities:		
	I found Q _____ easy.	I found Q _____ challenging.	I found Q _____ interesting.

1. Mr Miacca 'hoisted' Tommy over his shoulder. Tick the word with the most similar meaning.

   (a) lowered ☐   (b) lifted ☐   (c) lightened ☐

2. Write a Standard English version for each of these words.

   (a) 'erbs: __________   (b) 'em: __________   (c) 'usband: __________

3. Find the antonyms for these words in the text.

   (a) tender __________   (b) worried __________   (c) inconsiderate __________

   (d) good __________   (e) foolish __________   (f) tiny __________

4. Find the synonyms for these words in the text.

   (a) road __________   (b) scary __________   (c) enormous __________

   (d) barely __________   (e) dessert __________   (f) intelligent __________

5. Write homophones from the text for the words below.

   (a) buoy __________   (b) deer __________   (c) coarse __________

   (d) paws __________   (e) write __________

   (f) meet __________   (g) shore __________

   (h) sum __________   (i) hymn __________

   (j) eight __________   (k) knot __________

6. Find the words in the text that have these suffixes and add them to the table.

-ly		-ed	

My learning log	**Colour:**	I ⬡understand⬡ / ⬡need more practice on⬡ synonyms and antonyms.
		I ⬡can⬡ / ⬡can't⬡ recognise homophones.
		I ⬡can⬡ / ⬡can't⬡ recognise '-ly' and '-ed' suffixes.

The Legends of King Arthur's Swords – 1

Read these versions of the legends.

The Sword in the Stone

Young Arthur, who was a squire for his older brother Sir Kay the knight, was sent to collect his sword which they had left behind. Rushing back to the house, Arthur somehow got lost along the way. Frantically worried that he wouldn't hand Kay his sword in time for the games, Arthur had the great fortune to spot a sword jutting out from an anvil mounted on a rock.

Arthur glanced around but saw no one, and as he was an honest boy he knew he'd borrow the sword and return it when the games were finished. Heading over to the anvil, Arthur grabbed the sword's handle and struggled to remove it for a moment before it came free in his hands. Arthur rushed back to his brother with the sword but Kay became angry and asked Arthur why he'd brought him another sword and not his own. When Arthur explained the story, Kay ran to his father excitedly proclaiming, 'I am the new king!' A puzzled Arthur followed.

Sir Ector gazed at Kay suspiciously. 'Where'd you get this sword?' he demanded. Sensing the truth was the best answer, he told his father that Arthur had pulled it from the stone. At this, both men bowed down to Arthur and saluted him as their king.

With Arthur still looking puzzled, Sir Ector asked, 'Did you not read the inscription on the stone? It clearly says "HE WHO REMOVES THIS SWORD WILL BE THE RIGHTFUL KING OF THE LAND".'

From that moment on, Arthur's life would never be the same.

Excalibur

Many years later, after a difficult battle in which this sword was broken in half, Arthur and Merlin were travelling the country. Arthur was lamenting, 'What kind of King has no sword?'

He and Merlin soon came across a great lake where they noticed an unusual sight. From the lake rose a woman's hand, gripping the most dazzling sword Arthur had ever seen. A fair maiden then appeared out of the fog, walking towards them on the lake's surface.

'Here comes the Lady of the Lake', Merlin explained. 'The sword belongs to her and you must ask her if you can take it.'

The lady greeted Merlin and Arthur kindly and agreed to Arthur's request for the sword. She explained it was called Excalibur and would serve Arthur well. She directed the two to a boat on the lake's edge. The men got in and rowed to the sword, which the hand promptly released when Arthur took hold of it.

My learning log	When I read these legends, I could read:	☐ all of them. ☐ most of them. ☐ parts of them.

The Legends of King Arthur's Swords – 2 Comprehension

1. What is the purpose of these two texts?

____

2. (a) Choose and copy a phrase that captures your attention or interest.

____

   (b) Explain why you chose this phrase.

____

3. Write the location where each sword was found.

   SWORD 1: ____

   SWORD 2: ____

4. How would you describe the character of Sir Kay?

____

5. Which word, in paragraph two of the first legend, tells you that Arthur did not
   understand what it meant to have pulled the sword out of the stone?

   ____

6. What do you think Arthur did with Excalibur once he took it from the lake?

____

____

7. Why do you think direct speech was used in the texts?

____

8. What language feature on page 35 tells you that there are two different legends
   about Arthur?

____

9. What are the dictionary meanings of the following words?

   (a) frantically ____

   (b) anvil ____

   (c) lamenting ____

My learning log	While doing these activities:		
	I found Q _______ easy.	I found Q _______ challenging.	I found Q _______ interesting.

1. (a) Write the five words in the text with the suffix '-ly'.

___________ ___________ ___________ ___________ ___________

(b) If the root word ends with '-ic', '-ally' is added rather than just '-ly'. Which

word above has the suffix '-ally'? ___________

2. Write antonyms for the words in brackets to change the meaning.

(a) A puzzled Arthur (followed) ___________.

(b) The lady greeted Merlin and Arthur (kindly) ___________

and (agreed to) ___________ Arthur's request for the sword.

3. Write a synonym for each word below.

(a) puzzled ___________   (b) angry ___________

(c) collect ___________   (d) appeared ___________

4. (a) Circle the prefix that these words have in common.

remove   retrace   return

(b) What does this prefix mean? ___________

(c) Write a sentence using each word.

remove: ___________

retrace: ___________

return: ___________

5. Circle the words with the /ʌ/ sound spelt 'ou'; for example, touch, double.

young	mounted	country	house	trouble	cloud

6. Which words from the text are homophones for the following words?

(a) scent ___________   (b) weigh ___________

(c) hymn ___________   (d) witch ___________

My learning log	**Colour:**	I (understand) / (need more practice on) synonyms and antonyms. I (know) / (don't know) the meaning of the prefix 're-'. I (can) / (can't) recognise homophones.

Adjectives – 1

Adjectives are describing words.
They help make writing clearer and more interesting.

1. Read the paragraph about the dragonfly. Some of the nouns are in bold print. Highlight the adjectives that describe these nouns. (Hint: Ask 'What kind of?' in front of the noun.)

> *A dragonfly is a flying* **insect**. *It gets its scary* **name** *because it looks like a tiny* **dragon**. *However, a dragonfly is a gentle* **creature** *and does not bite or sting people. It can have a blue, red or green* **body** *and white, yellow or black* **markings**. *A dragonfly has compound* **eyes**, *large* **wings**, *and strong* **jaws** *and sharp* **teeth** *for crunching up other insects. It is most likely to be found near damp* **places**.

2. Use adjectives to answer the questions about the dragonfly.

   (a) What type of insect is it? _______________________________

   (b) What kind of name does it have? _______________________________

   (c) What colours can its body have? _______________________________

   ____

   (d) What colour markings can it have? _______________________________

   ____

   (e) Describe its jaws and its teeth. _______________________________

   (f) What kind of places can it be found? _______________________________

3. (a) Unjumble the words below. The first letter is in bold print.

   (i) o**l**ng _______________   (ii) rma**w** _______________

   (iii) **l**lcao _______________   (iv) **y**ic _______________

   (v) **z**lay _______________   (vi) hily**c**l _______________

   (b) The words above can be used as adjectives. Use them to fill in the missing words in these sentences.

   (i) Our _______________ dog is getting too fat and needs to be

   taken on _______________ walks in the _______________ park.

   (ii) The _______________ wind was coming off the _______________

   mountain and made us huddle around the _______________ fire.

Adjectives – 2

Adjectives are describing words. They help make writing clearer and more interesting for the reader.

The answers to the clues for the crossword puzzle are words that can be used as adjectives. Use the crossword to help you work out the answers.

Across

2. The ________________ boy tripped over his shoelaces.

4. We often see ________________ crows feeding on the riverbank.

6. As it was a ________________ day, we stayed indoors.

9. The ________________ dog lapped up the water greedily.

10. The truck was too ________________ to fit in the garage.

12. The ________________ baby was woken by the door banging.

Down

1. A fox has a ________________ tail.

2. A peacock has ________________ feathers.

3. The ________________ giraffe easily reached the topmost branch.

4. The ________________ ants hurried into their nest.

5. The ________________ child held the door open for the old lady.

7. We all jumped when we heard the ________________ noise.

8. Our bedroom was ________________ so we spent two hours tidying it.

11. ________________ shoes often cause blisters.

Learn from Home Workbook 4   978-1-912760-64-0   www.prim-ed.com   Prim-Ed Publishing

Banana and choc chip muffins

This recipe will make 12 banana choc chip muffins.

Ingredients

- 2 cups self raising flour
- 1/3 cup sugar
- 1 cup choc chips
- 60 g margarine plus extra for greasing
- 300 mL milk
- 3 eggs
- 1 teaspoon vanilla essence
- 2 soft bananas

Equipment

- large bowl
- microwave safe jug
- medium bowl
- fork
- sieve
- measuring cups
- measuring spoons
- wooden spoon
- muffin tray – 12 muffins

Method

1. Preheat oven to 210 °Celsius.
2. Grease muffin tray with margarine.
3. Sieve flour into large bowl.
4. Add sugar and choc chips.
5. Melt margarine in a microwave safe jug.
6. Add milk to the melted margarine and stir.
7. Break eggs into cup, making sure there is no shell.
8. Add eggs to milk mix and whisk with fork to combine.
9. Mash bananas with fork in smaller bowl.
10. Stir mashed banana and vanilla essence into milk mix.
11. Make a well in flour and add milk mix.
12. Gently combine mixture with wooden spoon. Do not over mix, or muffins will not be light!
13. Cook on top shelf in oven for about 15 to 20 minutes, until golden.
14. Test that muffins are cooked by gently touching the top of one. (Make sure your hands are clean!) Muffin should spring back.
15. Ask an adult to remove muffins from oven. Allow to cool.

Now test your muffins by tasting them!

Use the procedure on page 27 to complete the page.

1. Title

The recipe is for which type of muffins?

2. Goal

Complete the sentence. The goal of the recipe is to make

3. Materials

Draw two of the ingredients and two pieces of equipment. Label them.

4. Method

(a) Write the number of each step in the box.

(i)   Mash bananas with fork in smaller bowl.

(ii) Add sugar and choc chips.

(iii) Ask an adult to remove muffins from oven. Allow to cool.

(iv) Make a well in flour and add milk mix.

(v)   Set oven to 210 °Celsius.

(vi) Cook on top shelf in oven for about 15 to 20 minutes, until golden.

(b) Explain why the order of the steps is important.

____

____

(c) Complete the sentence.

Each step of the method begins with a

c_______________ I_______________

and ends in a f_______________

s_______________.

5. Test

How will you know if you have followed this procedure well?

1. Plan and write a procedure for a recipe you know well or for a different type of muffin (e.g. instead of banana choc chip, it could be carrot and walnut.)

Title

Goal

Ingredients

Equipment

Method

Numbered and in order

Test

How will you test if your recipe works?

2. Write your procedure.

3. Edit your work.

Swimming gold!

Read the recount.

saturday 15 march: today has been the best day of the year so far for me the club swimming championships were held and for the first time i was a competitor i was both excited and scared, all at the same time

my event was the 200-metre individual medley as i climbed on to the block and waited for the starter's gun, i imagined i was in an olympic final i knew i wasn't the fastest over 50 metres in any of the individual strokes, but with the four of them together, i had a good chance of winning my dive felt perfect and i was under way each stroke felt smooth and strong, but i believe it was the hours i spent practising my turns that really made the difference in less than four minutes, the gold was mine

❶ Punctuation

(a) The recount needs 21 capital letters and 9 full stops.

(b) How many capital letters are used for:

  (i) sentence beginnings? _____

  (ii) the pronoun 'I'? _____

  (iii) proper nouns? _____

(c) Circle all the commas. How many are there? _____

(d) Circle the colon.

❷ Spelling

Some words have silent letters; e.g. **k***new.*

(a) Write in the missing letter.

Silent 'b'	Silent 'k'	Silent 'g'	Silent 'n'
clim___	___now	___nome	autum___
thum___	___night	___nat	colum___
lam___	___neel	___narled	hym___

❸ Grammar

The past tense of verbs is often formed by adding 'ed' to the word.

(a) Underline the 5 verbs with the past tense formed this way.

(b) In the text, find the past tense of these verbs.

  (i) to hold _______________

  (ii) to know _______________

  (iii) to have _______________

  (iv) to feel _______________

  (v) to spend _______________

Pronouns are used in place of nouns. In this text, the pronoun 'I' is used many times as the writer is talking about herself.

(c) What are the other 3 pronouns she uses when talking about herself?

_______________ _______________

____

     Learn from Home Workbook 4   978-1-912760-64-0   www.prim-ed.com   Prim-Ed Publishing

Dinosaur feast

Read the narrative poem.

the dinosaur moved threw the forest ________________

he snifed the air to the west ________________

he spotted his goal—a heard of beasts, ________________

enjoying their own grassy feest ________________

he lowered hiz head and started to run, ________________

on gigantic, boney feet ________________

his gapping jaws took aim and soon, ________________

the pray was his to eat ________________

a bite or too and then the hunter, ________________

began his own meety feast ________________

❶ Punctuation

(a) The narrative poem needs 10 capital letters (one at the beginning of each line) and 6 full stops.

❷ Spelling

(a) Write the misspelt words correctly at the end of each line.

❸ Grammar

Pronouns are words used instead of nouns; for example, 'she', 'it', 'they', 'you'.

(a) Circle 3 different pronouns which can be found in the poem.

Conjunctions are words which join words, groups of words and sentences. They include words such as: and, because, so, if, when, that, as soon as.

(b) Write the joining word used in the poem.

____

(c) Write the two small sentences which make up this sentence.

'He lowered his head and started to run.'

____

____

Collective nouns are the names given to particular groups.

(d) What collective noun is given to the group of beasts in the poem?

____

❹ Vocabulary

(a) Find opposites in the text for these words.

(i)   east ______________________

(ii) tiny ______________________

(iii) finished ______________________

(iv) raised ______________________

Volcanoes

Read the explanation.

volcanoes are places on the earths surface (through/threw) (witch/which) molten rock, called magma, and gas from far below the surface erupt

volcanic eruptions can be violent, spilling hot lava ash dust gas and cinders over large areas

they can trigger tsunamis earthquakes floods rockfalls and mudflows eruptions have caused (some/sum) of the worst disasters in (historie/history), (killing/kiling) thousands of people

categories of volcanoes include: active dormant (sleeping) and extinct (no longer active)

every time a volcano erupts it becomes bigger, because as the lava cools it forms a (knew/new) layer of rock

although our understanding of volcanoes has increased, predicting (when/wen) they will erupt and limiting the damage they (corse/cause) is still difficult

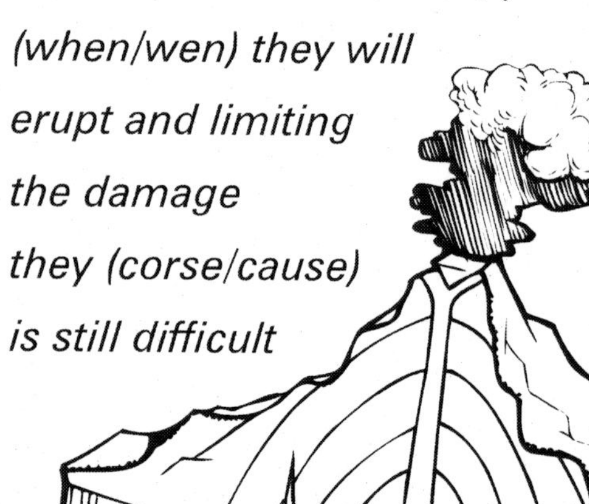

❶ Punctuation

(a) The explanation needs 8 capital letters, 7 full stops, 7 commas to separate items in a list and 1 apostrophe for possession.

(b) Circle the colon.

❷ Spelling

(a) Cross out the incorrectly spelt words.

When singular words are made plural, we can add 's' or 'es'; e.g. 'plants', 'potatoes'.

(b) Write the plural for these words.

   (i)   volcano _______________

   (ii) disaster _______________

   (iii) eruption _______________

❸ Grammar

(a) Change these present tense verbs used in the explanation to the past tense.

Present tense	Past tense
(i) erupt	
(ii) include	
(iii) cause	
(iv) trigger	
(v) are	
(vi) becomes	

(b) Write these verbs in the future tense.

   (i)   cause _______________________

   (ii) cools _______________________

   (iii) forms _______________________

   (iv) are   _______________________

PLACE VALUE

1. Write the numbers represented by the place value blocks. The first one is done for you.

	Thousands	Hundreds	Tens	Ones	Number
					1375
(a)					
(b)					
(c)					
(d)					

2. Write the value of the number that is underlined.

(a) <u>5</u>690 ___________________

(b) 39<u>7</u>1 ___________________

(c) 874<u>6</u> ___________________

(d) 45<u>3</u>1 ___________________

(e) <u>4</u>13 ___________________

(f) 74<u>8</u> ___________________

(g) 2<u>5</u>02 ___________________

(h) 9<u>0</u>67 ___________________

(i) <u>6</u>723 ___________________

(j) <u>4</u>025 ___________________

CHALLENGE

On the back of the sheet, draw this number using place value blocks (remember the thousand block is a cube): 1358.

Objective   *Recognises and demonstrates place value.*

EXPANDED NOTATION

1. Expand these numbers with written words.
   For example, 3529 = 3 thousands, 5 hundreds, 2 tens and 9 ones.

   (a) 4527 = ____

   (b) 319 = ____

   (c) 5201 = ____

   (d) 9746 = ____

   (e) 3081 = ____

   (f) 1452 = ____

2. Expand these with numbers.
   For example, 5603 = 5000 + 600 + 3.

   (a) 712 = _____________________   (b) 1637 = _____________________

   (c) 6572 = _____________________   (d) 2398 = _____________________

   (e) 8093 = _____________________   (f) 3214 = _____________________

   (g) 5805 = _____________________   (h) 7635 = _____________________

3. Rename these numbers.
   For example, 7645 = 7 x 1000 + 6 x 100 + 4 x 10 + 5 x 1

   (a) 4712 = _________ x 1000 + _________ x 100 + _________ x 10 + _________ x 1

   (b) 7903 = _________ x 1000 + _________ x 100 + _________ x 10 + _________ x 1

   (c) 1274 = _________ x 1000 + _________ x 100 + _________ x 10 + _________ x 1

   (d) 9685 = _________ x 1000 + _________ x 100 + _________ x 10 + _________ x 1

   (e) 5061 = _________ x 1000 + _________ x 100 + _________ x 10 + _________ x 1

4. Write the missing numbers.

   (a) 5000 + _______ + 80 + _______ = 5487   (b) _______ + 300 + _______ + 1 = 6341

   (c) _______ + _______ + 0 + _______ = 8509   (d) _______ + _______ + _______ + 5 = 3925

CHALLENGE

Write the number for these expanded numbers:

(a) 60 000 + 3000 + 400 + 60 + 7 = _______________

(b) 20 000 + 4000 + 800 + 30 + 9 = _______________

Objective   *Identifies and represents different forms of the same number.*

+/− INVERSES

1. When adding, numbers can be placed in any order and still give the same answer; e.g. $3 + 5 = 8$ is the same as $5 + 3 = 8$. Solve these addition facts, and then change the numbers around.

   (a) $4 + 3 =$ _____ $3 + 4 =$ _____   (b) $7 + 5 =$ _____   _____ + _____ = _____

   (c) $9 + 6 =$ _____   _____ + _____ = _____   (d) $8 + 4 =$ _____   _____ + _____ = _____

   (e) $7 + 6 =$ _____   _____ + _____ = _____   (f) $11 + 5 =$ _____   _____ + _____ = _____

   (g) $9 + 3 =$ _____   _____ + _____ = _____   (h) $14 + 2 =$ _____   _____ + _____ = _____

   (i) $23 + 15 =$ _____   _____ + _____ = _____   (j) $32 + 16 =$ _____   _____ + _____ = _____

> **However, subtraction cannot be done in any order; for example, $5 − 3$ does not give the same answer as $3 − 5$.**
>
> $5 − 3 = \boxed{2}$ but $3 − 5 = \boxed{-2}$

2. Addition and subtraction are related. Solve these addition and subtraction facts.

   (a) $6 + 8 =$ _____   so $14 − 6 =$ _____   (b) $5 + 4 =$ _____   so _____ − _____ = _____

   (c) $4 + 7 =$ _____   so _____ − _____ = _____   (d) $9 + 6 =$ _____   so _____ − _____ = _____

   (e) $12 + 14 =$ _____   so _____ − _____ = _____   (f) $23 + 16 =$ _____ so _____ − _____ = _____

   (g) $18 − 7 =$ _____   so $7 + 11 =$ _____   (h) $9 − 5 =$ _____   so _____ + _____ = _____

   (i) $10 − 3 =$ _____   so _____ + _____ = _____   (j) $16 − 4 =$ _____   so _____ + _____ = _____

   (k) $28 − 12 =$ _____   so _____ + _____ = _____   (l) $35 − 10 =$ _____ so _____ + _____ = _____

3. Draw lines to match the related addition and subtraction facts.

   (a) $5 + 3 = 8$ $12 + 3 = 15$ $36 − 24 = 12$ $9 − 7 = 2$

   (b) $2 + 7 = 9$ $19 - 13 = 6$ $1 + 8 = 9$ $36 − 12 = 24$

   (c) $15 − 3 = 12$ $3 + 5 = 8$ $15 − 12 = 3$ $8 + 1 = 9$

   (d) $9 − 8 = 1$ $24 + 12 = 36$ $7 + 2 = 9$ $8 − 3 = 5$

   (e) $12 + 24 = 36$ $9 − 2 = 7$ $8 − 5 = 3$ $6 + 13 = 19$

   (f) $19 - 6 = 13$ $9 − 1 = 8$ $13 + 6 = 19$ $3 + 12 = 15$

CHALLENGE

Write four number facts using the numbers 4, 5 and 9.

Objectives • *Understands addition can be done in any order but subtraction cannot.*
• *Understands addition and subtraction are inverse operations.*

CHECKING CALCULATIONS

1. Check the total of several numbers by adding in reverse order.

   (a) 3 + 5 + 8 = _________ and 8 + 5 + 3 = _________

   (b) 2 + 7 + 9 = _________ and _________ + _________ + _________ = _________

   (c) 10 + 5 + 8 = _________ and _________ + _________ + _________ = _________

   (d) 12 + 8 + 4 = _________ and _________ + _________ + _________ = _________

2. Work out the answers. Match to equivalent calculations.

   (a) 25 – 10 = _________   •   •   17 – 8 = _________

   (b) 10 + 10 = _________   •   •   5 + 5 + 5 = _________

   (c) 8 + 9 = _________   •   •   Double 4 = _________

   (d) 4 + 4 + 4 = _________   •   •   35 – 15 = _________

   (e) 2 + 4 + 2 = _________   •   •   16 + 7 = _________

   (f) 23 – 7 = _________   •   •   20 - 8 = _________

3. Estimate answers by rounding to the nearest 10.

   (a) 23 + 17 = __40__   (b) 29 – 7 = __22__   (c) 53 + 39 = __92__

       20 + 20 = _______   _______ - _______ = _______   _______ + _______ = _______

4. Estimate answers by rounding to the nearest 100.

   (a) 298 + 503 = __801__   (b) 804 – 375 = __429__   (c) 914 + 283 = __1197__

       300 + 500 = _______   _______ - _______ = _______   _______ + _______ = _______

5. Estimate answers by rounding to the nearest 1000.

   (a) 4851 + 2361 = __7212__   (b) 6329 – 1694 = __4635__   (c) 2795 + 7014 = __9809__

       _______ + _______ = _______   _______ - _______ = _______   _______ + _______ = _______

CHALLENGE

Write an equivalent calculation for each of these sums.

(a) 99 – 22 = 77   (b) 35 + 43 = 78   (c) Double 60 = 120

Objective   *Uses a range of strategies to check calculations.*

EQUIVALENT UNITS OF TIME

M Measurement

1. Complete these statements.

   (a) There are ________ seconds in one minute.
   (b) There are ________ minutes in one hour.
   (c) There are ________ hours in one day.
   (d) There are ________ days in one week.
   (e) There are between ________ and ________ days in one month.
   (f) There are between ________ and ________ days in one year.
   (g) There are ________ weeks in one year.
   (h) There are ________ months in one year.

2. Write the seven units of time in order of size, from largest to smallest.

day	**hour**	**minute**	**month**	**second**	**week**	**year**

largest → ________, ________, ________, ________,

________, ________, ________ → smallest.

3. Match the equivalent measurements.

½ day	2 minutes	½ hour	26 weeks	30 seconds	2 hours
30 minutes	½ year	12 hours	120 seconds	120 minutes	½ minute

4. Convert the times.

   (a) ________ seconds = 3 minutes
   (b) 2 minutes = ________ seconds
   (c) ________ minutes = 2 hours
   (d) ½ hour = ________ minutes
   (e) ________ hours = 2 days
   (f) 3 days = ________ hours
   (g) ________ weeks = 28 days
   (h) 21 days = ________ weeks
   (i) ________ weeks = 2 years
   (j) 3 years = ________ weeks
   (k) ________ months = 4 years
   (l) 2 years = ________ months

CHALLENGE

Solve the word problems.

(a) Casey went to Australia for six weeks. John went for 38 days.

Who went for the longer amount of time? ________ For how many days longer? ________

(b) Three friends made a cake. Tina spent 0.5 hours, Priya 34 minutes and Ben 1500 seconds. Write the times from shortest to longest.

________, ________, ________

Objective *Knows equivalent units of time and converts between them.*

PERIMETER – FORMAL UNITS

1. Record the perimeter of these shapes by counting the centimetre squares around the edges.

(a) 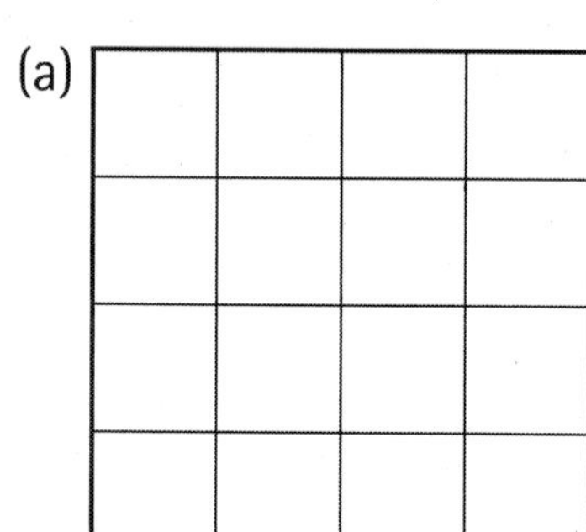

_______ cm

(b) 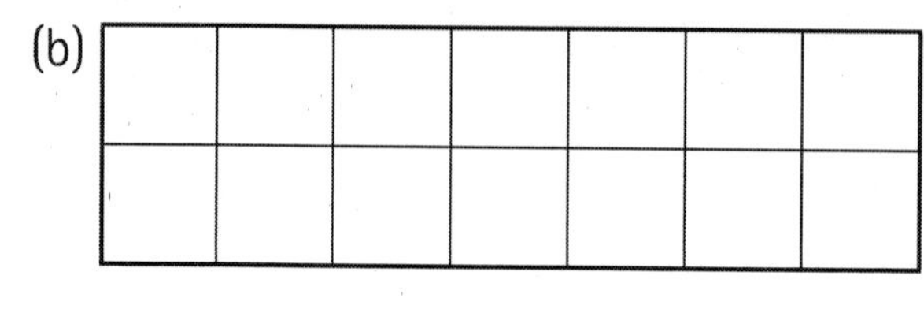

_______ cm

(c) 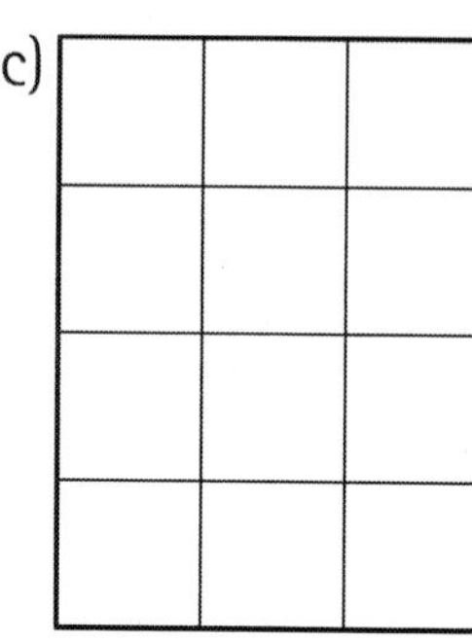

_______ cm

2. Calculate the perimeter of these shapes.

(a) _______ cm

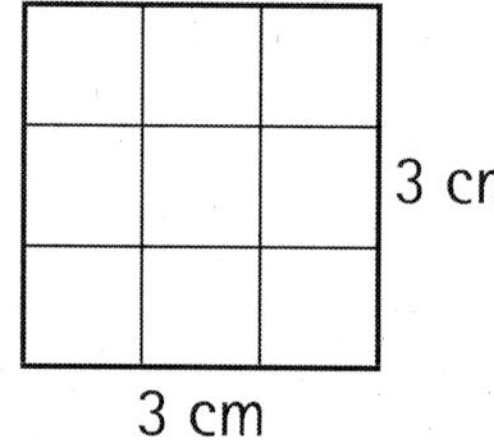
3 cm
3 cm

(b) _______ cm

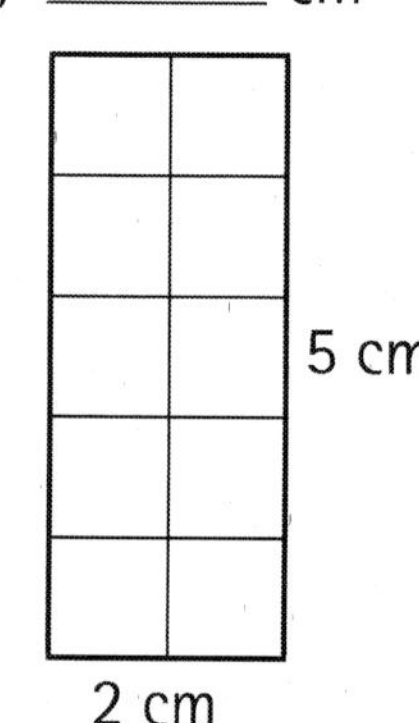
5 cm
2 cm

(c) _______ cm

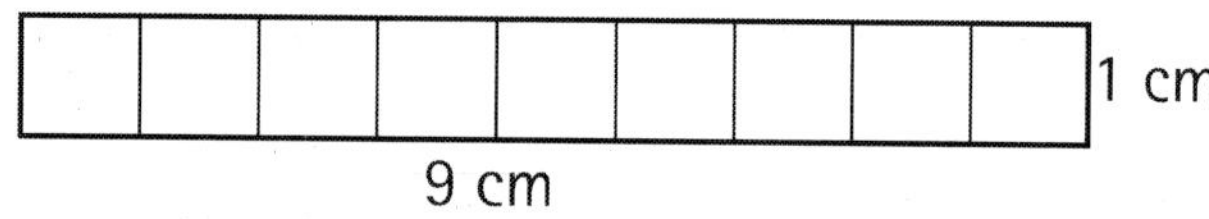
1 cm
9 cm

(d) _______ m

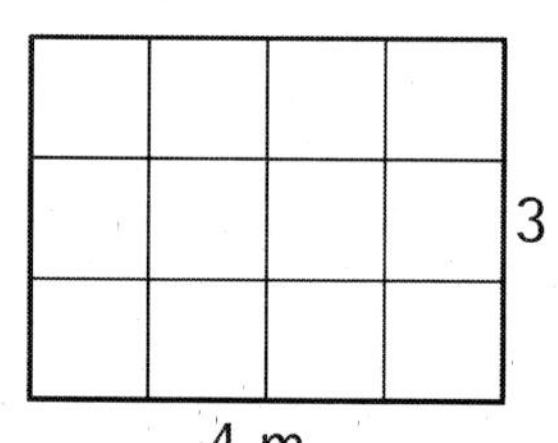
3 m
4 m

(e) _______ m

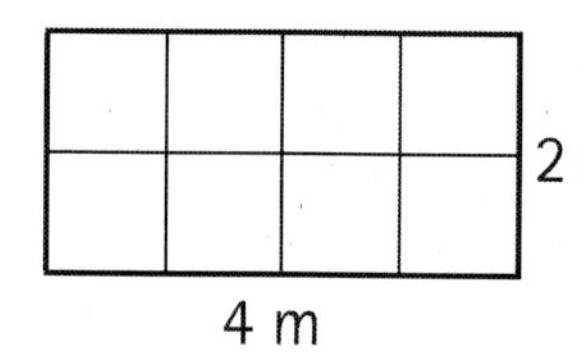
2 m
4 m

(f) _______ m

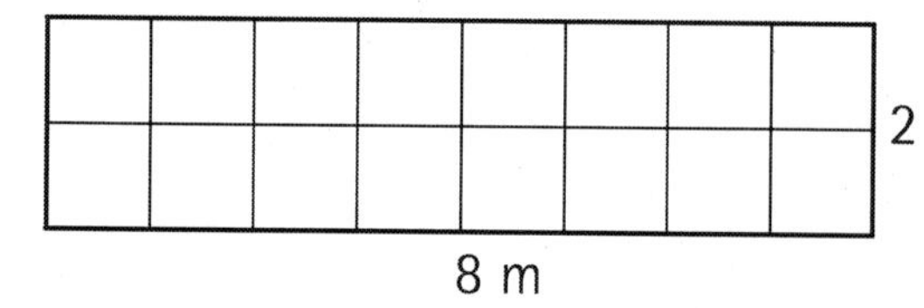
2 m
8 m

CHALLENGE Measure each side of these shapes in centimetres and then find the perimeter.

(a) 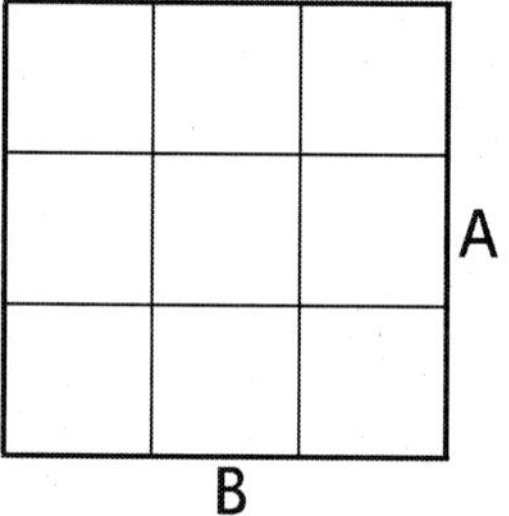
A
B

side A = _______ cm

side B = _______ cm

perimeter = _______ cm

(b) 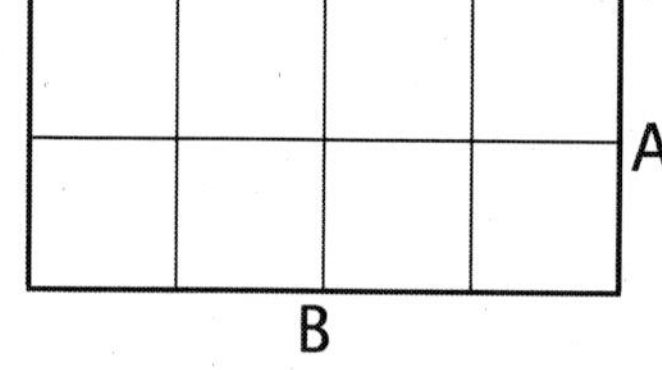
A
B

side A = _______ cm

side B = _______ cm

perimeter = _______ cm

(c) 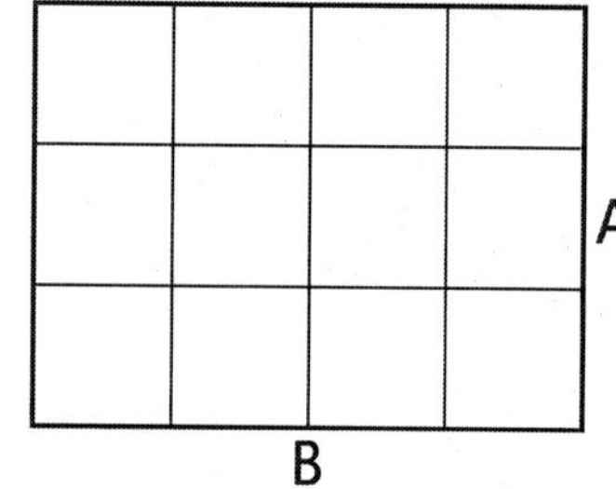
A
B

side A = _______ cm

side B = _______ cm

perimeter = _______ cm

Objective	Measures the perimeter of objects in centimetres and metres.

 Learn from Home Workbook 4   978-1-912760-64-0   www.prim-ed.com   Prim-Ed Publishing

ANGLES

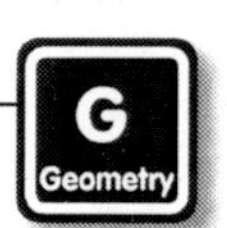

Angles can be found everywhere, especially right angles, which are the most common. When a horizontal and vertical line join (perpendicular lines) they form a right angle at the corner.

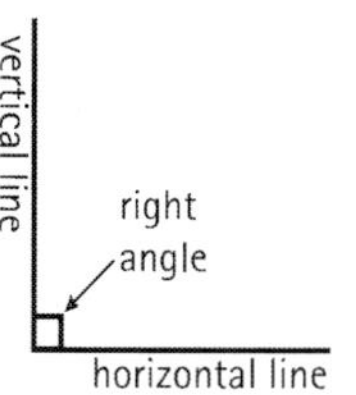

1. Find and draw three right angles in the classroom.

<table>
<tr><td>(a)</td><td>(b)</td><td>(c)</td></tr>
</table>

A right angle is 90°. A straight angle (two right angles) is 180°.
Half a right angle is 45°.

2. Trace over the right angles in red. Trace the straight line angles in yellow and the half-right angles in blue.

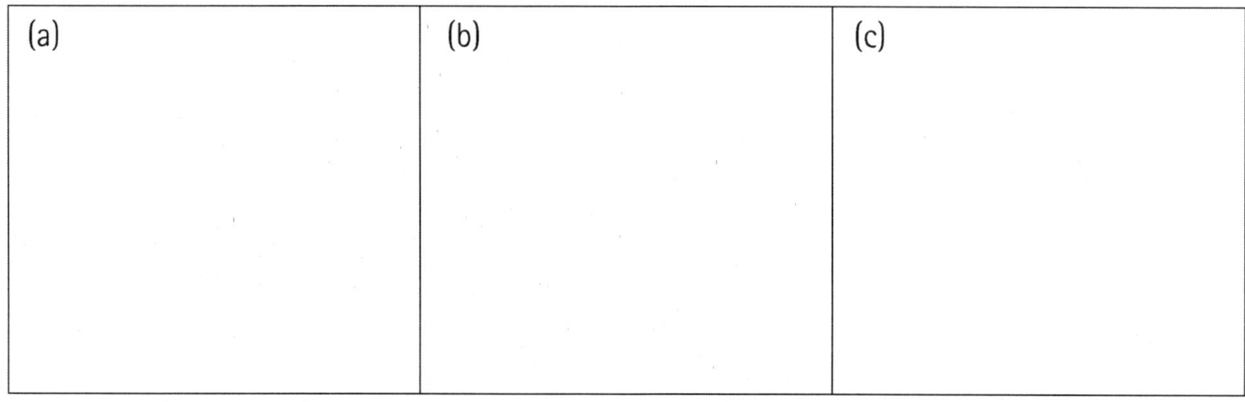

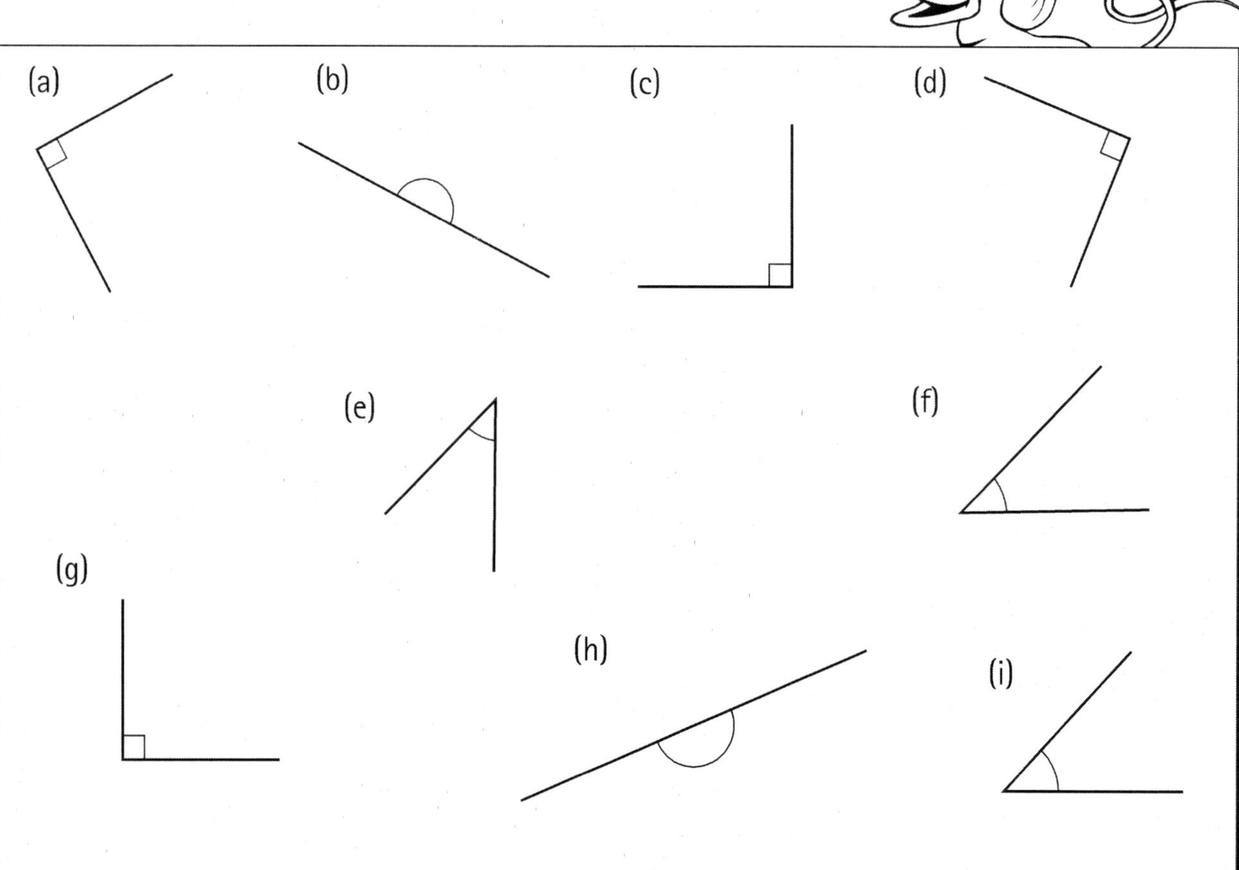

CHALLENGE
On the back of this sheet, draw and write the name of a shape that has four right angles.

Objective   *Recognises and describes angles represented in the environment.*

IDENTIFYING ANGLES

An angle can be found where two lines meet.

The right angle (90°) is the most common angle found.

The 180° angle is also common.

The 45° angle is half a right angle.

Angles are measured by the amount of space between the lines.

1. Look at the picture below and locate these angles.

   (a) Trace over the right angles in red.

   (b) Trace over the 45° angles in blue.

   (c) Trace over the 180° angles in green.

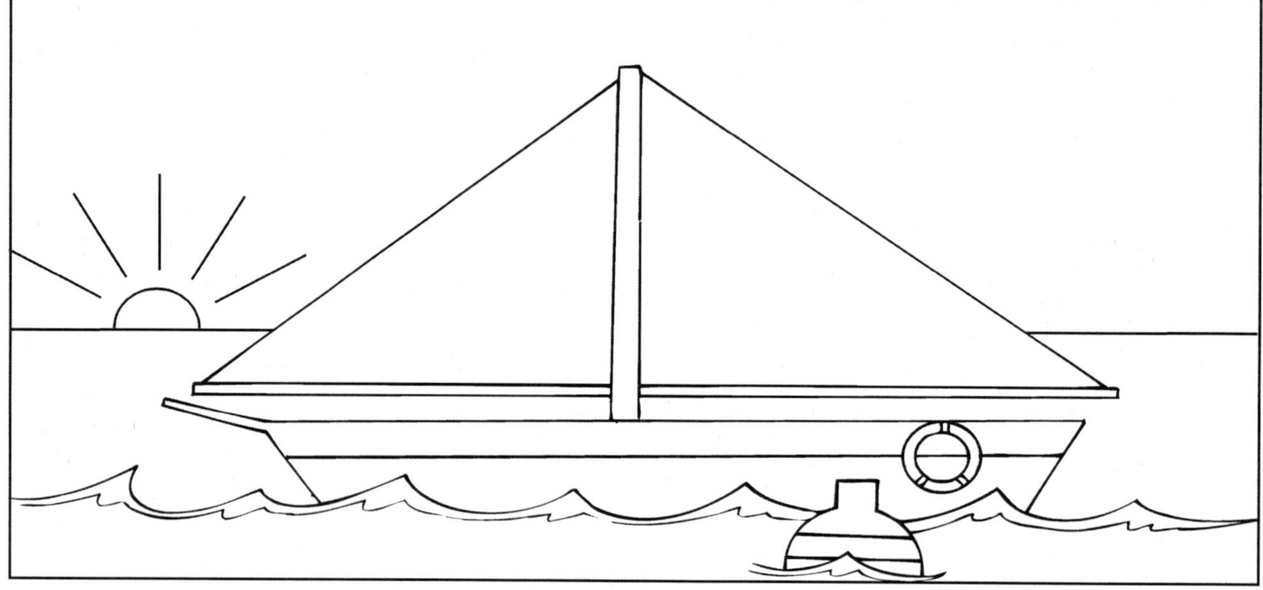

2. Colour the shapes with right angles red.

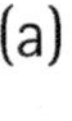

(a) 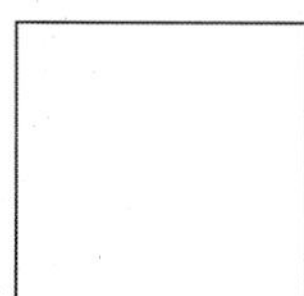   (b) 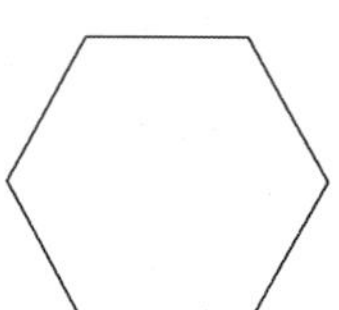   (c) 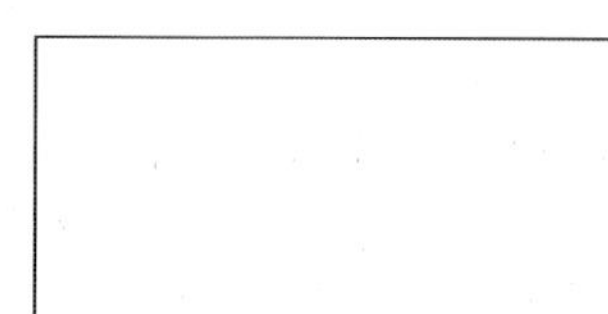   (d) 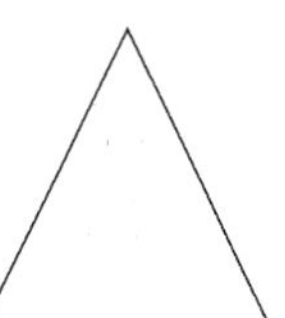

(e) 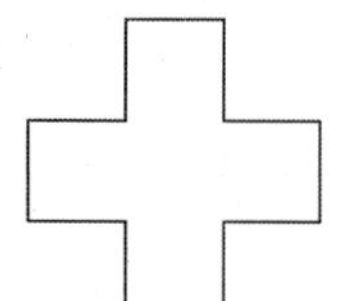   (f) 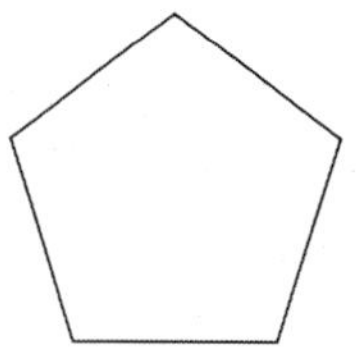   (g) 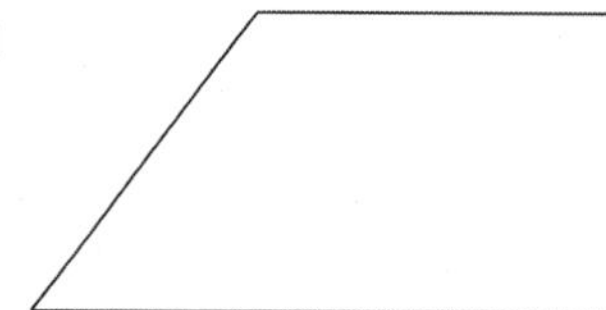   (h) 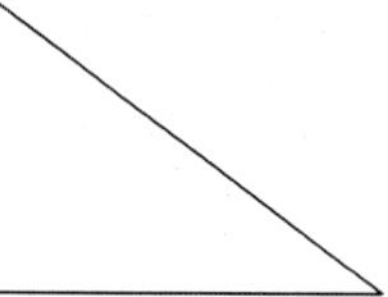

CHALLENGE

List the 180° angles you can see in the classroom.

Objective *Identifies angles in 2-D shapes and in the environment.*

Choosing materials

Materials are chosen to make something because they have properties which suit what that object is used for.

1 Study these objects and say why they have been made out of the materials used. The first one has been done for you. Add one of your own.

Object	Made of …	Why was the main material chosen?
pencil	wood, paint, lead	easily sharpened, light, strong
soft drink bottle		
window		
shirt		

2 How well did each material soak up water? Test each to find out.

Material	Rate out of 5 (1 = hopeless, 5 = great)	Comment on how good it is
tissue paper	1 2 3 4 5	
newspaper	1 2 3 4 5	
magazine paper	1 2 3 4 5	
aluminium foil	1 2 3 4 5	
writing paper	1 2 3 4 5	
paper towel	1 2 3 4 5	

3 (a) What material(s) rated best? _______________________

(b) Why? _______________________

4 (a) Which material was worst? _______________________

(b) Why? _______________________

Materials to make a home

1 Match the animal to its home.

(a) hermit crab •   • lodge

(b) beaver •   • nest

(c) bee •   • burrow

(d) squirrel •   • shell

(e) mole •   • hive

2 List some natural materials that animal homes are made from.

3 (a) What manufactured materials are used to build our homes?

(b) What properties do you think materials used to build homes should have?

4 Design a house for a 'mini' person to live in. Make sure it can stand up to all types of weather.

My plan and materials.

Why did you choose those materials?

How could you improve your house?

Changing by heating

When we heat a substance it changes from the way
it looked before.

- Draw and write about what each of these substances
  looked like when it had been heated.

- Use these words to complete each sentence.

chip   toast   melted   hard-boiled

Before	After
(a) An egg	The egg became _____________.
(b) A slice of bread.	The bread became _____________.
(c) A slice of potato	The potato became a _____________.
(d) Butter	The butter _____________.

WEEK 4

ENGLISH

MATHEMATICS

SCIENCE

World Climatic Zones – 1

Read the explanation.

Climate is the average weather of a place over many years. Climatic zones differ around the world. They have an impact on the types of vegetation (flora), the weather, the animals (fauna) and the daily lives of people in the region. The climate of a place is affected by:

Latitude

Lines of latitude (invisible lines running horizontally across the earth's surface) tell us how far a place is from the equator (0°). Places close to the equator experience similar, warm temperatures year round. This is because the sun's rays are dispersed over larger areas of land as you move away from the equator. Additionally, polar regions are colder because the sun's rays have further to travel compared to Equatorial regions.

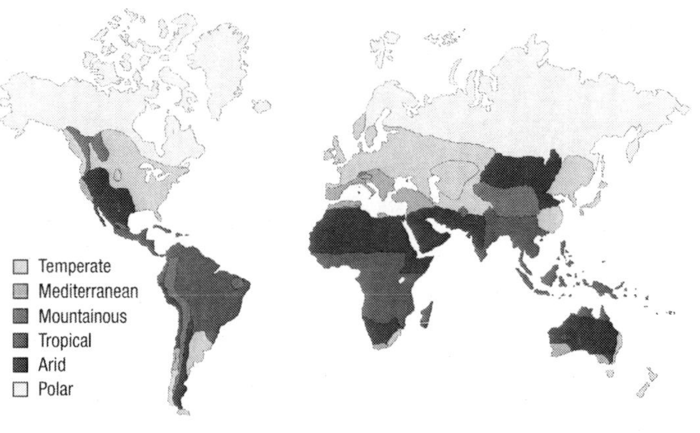

Altitude

Altitude means height above sea level. Places that are at high altitudes experience cooler weather as the air is thinner (less dense) and cannot hold heat as easily.

Winds

Winds that blow from cold areas will lower temperatures and winds that blow from hot areas will increase temperatures. Winds from the sea often bring rain.

Distance from the sea

Landmasses heat up and cool down more quickly than the sea. Therefore, coastal regions have a lower temperature range (difference between lowest and highest) than inland areas. Coastal areas experience milder winters and cooler summers compared with the colder winters and hotter summers of inland territories. Coastal areas are also wetter as the moisture from the sea (which forms clouds) often evaporates before it reaches inland.

Ocean currents

Currents transport warm water and precipitation (rain) from the equator north and south towards the poles and cold water from the poles back to the tropics. Without currents, temperatures would be more extreme—very hot at the equator and much colder towards the poles.

My learning log	When I read this explanatory text, I could read: ☐ all of it. ☐ most of it. ☐ parts of it.

World Climatic Zones – 2

1. Which language features are included in the text? Tick them.

   - an opening paragraph ☐
   - bullet points ☐
   - paragraphs of information ☐
   - maps and images ☐
   - a table sorting information ☐
   - lines that end in rhyming words ☐
   - the words 'Once upon a time ...' and '... they lived happily ever after' ☐

2. Write five things that affect the climate of a place.

   ____

3. Use words from the text to give the meanings of the following words and phrases.

   (a) flora _______________________   (b) fauna _______________________

   (c) less dense _______________________   (d) precipitation _______________________

   (e) lines of latitude _______________________

   (f) altitude _______________________

4. The word 'dispersed' means _______________________.

5. What causes cooler weather at high altitudes?

   ____

6. Which regions get more rain—coastal or inland regions? Explain why.

   ____

   ____

7. Choose one paragraph that was difficult to understand. Write one question that will give you more information and help you understand it.

   ____

8. What do you think would happen if polar regions were suddenly tilted closer to the sun?

   ____

   ____

My learning log	While doing these activities:		
	I found Q _____ easy.	I found Q _____ challenging.	I found Q _____ interesting.

World Climatic Zones – 3

1. Use a dictionary to find the difference between each pair of words.

(a) affected ____

     effected ____

(b) current ____

     currant ____

2. (a) Use a dictionary to find out the origin and meaning of the word 'transport'.

____

(b) Write two other words that begin with 'trans-'.

________________   ________________

3. Underline the suffix in each word below.

evaporates	colder	dispersed	climatic
precipitation	thinner	temperatures	territories	hotter

4. (a) Circle the suffix that these words have in common.

> quickly   horizontally   easily   accidentally

(b) If the root word ends in a consonant and 'y', the 'y' is changed to 'i'. (Only if the word has more than one syllable!)

Which word above follows this rule? ________________

What is this word's root word? ________________

5. Write the root word for each word below.

(a) equatorial ________________   (b) horizontally ________________

(c) additionally ________________   (d) polar ________________

6. (a) Find and write a word from the text with the suffix '-ture'. ________________

(b) Write this word in a sentence.

____

My learning log	**Colour:**	I [can] / [can't] recognise homophones and near-homophones.
		I [know] / [don't know] the origins and meanings of words.
		I [understand] / [need more practice on] suffixes.

Great British Artists – 1

Read the explanation in the flow chart.

There is no doubt that Britain has produced some of the greatest artists in the world. Read short biographies of three of them.

Thomas Gainsborough (1727–1788)

- Landscape and portrait painter
- Born in Sudbury, Suffolk, son of a weaver
- 1740 – studied engraving in London
- 1769 – founding member of Royal Academy
- 1769 – exhibited portraits of well-known or notorious people
- 1780 – painted portraits of King George III and his queen; became Royal Family's favourite painter
- Established 18th century British landscape school
- Merged figures in portraits with landscape; painted from observations of nature rather than formal rules of art
- Most famous paintings – *Girl with Pigs* (1781–2), *The Blue Boy* (1770) and *Portrait of Mrs Graham* (1775)

John Constable (1776–1837)

- Oil and watercolour landscape painter
- Born in East Bergholt, Suffolk, son of a merchant
- 1799 – studied at Royal Academy
- 1819 – first important painting – *The White Horse* sold
- Inspired by Thomas Gainsborough
- Developed techniques of brilliant colour and lively brushwork to show light and movement of clouds and the sky
- Lectured at Royal Academy
- Painted large scale landscapes called 'six footers' with full-scale preliminary oil sketches
- Most famous paintings—*Dedham Vale* (1802) and *The Hay Wain* (1821)

J.M.W. Turner (1775–1851)

- Landscape painter, water colourist and printmaker
- Born Covent Garden, London, son of a barber and wig maker
- 1785 – First engraved plates done
- 1786 – Sketched town and surroundings of Margate
- 1789 – Pencil sketches of Berkshire landscape
- Drew for architects and topographical draughtsmen
- 1789 – Entered Royal Academy aged 14; first exhibit at 15
- 1796 – First oil painting – *Fishermen at Sea* – exhibited
- Called the 'Painter of Light'; painted shipwrecks, fires, storms, sunlight, rain, fog, natural catastrophes
- Most famous paintings – *The Fighting Temeraire* (1839) and *Snow Storm* (1842)

My learning log	When I read these biographies, I could read: ☐ all of them. ☐ most of them. ☐ parts of them.

Great British Artists – 2

1. The purpose of the texts is to ___________________________

____.

2. Name six common things that are recorded in the biography of each artist.

____

____

____

3. Write one sentence about the painting style (the way each painted) of each artist.

• Gainsborough ___________________________

____

• Constable ___________________________

____

• Turner ___________________________

____

4. Write the dictionary meaning of each word.

(a) inspired   ___________________________

(b) notorious   ___________________________

(c) preliminary   ___________________________

(d) topographical ___________________________

5. Why do you think Gainsborough painted portraits of well-known or notorious people in his early career?

____

6. Why were bullet points used for the main part of the text?

____

7. Which two artists both did engravings?

____

My learning log	While doing these activities:		
	I found Q ______ easy.	I found Q ______ challenging.	I found Q ______ interesting.

Great British Artists – 3

1. Write six words from the text that relate to art and painting.

_________ _________ _________ _________ _________ _________

2. Write eight words that are occupations of the 18th and 19th centuries.

_________________ _________________ _________________ _________________

_________________ _________________ _________________ _________________

3. Underline the synonym for each word.

    (a) **favourite:**   taste   best-liked   worst

    (b) **lively:**   energetic   friendly   quiet

    (c) **observations:**   stubborn   studies   ideas

4. In the phrase 'natural catastrophes', which antonym could be used to replace 'catastrophes' to give it the opposite meaning? Circle it.

    disasters   good fortune   emergencies   climate

5. Find and write seven compound words in the text.

_________ _________ _________ _________

_________ _________ _________

6. (a) Find and write a word with the /k/ sound spelt 'que'. ______________

    (b) Can you think of any other words with this ending?

    ____

7. Write two words in the text with the suffix '-ous'.

_________________   _________________

8. Use a dictionary to find the origin of the word 'preliminary' and explain what the prefix 'pre-' means in the word.

____

____

My learning log	Colour:	I [can] / [can't] sort words by topic.
		I [understand] / [need more practice on] synonyms and antonyms.
		I [know] / [don't know] about compound words.

Comparing things

When we compare two people or things we change the *adjective*, usually by adding *er*; for example: *'This tree is tall but that tree is taller'*.

When we compare three or more people or things we change the adjective, usually by adding *est*; for example: *'This tree is tall but that tree is taller. The tree over there is the tallest'*.

1. Use the adjectives below to complete the paragraph. You will have to change the words by adding *er* or *est* to them.

> **wavy**   **cheeky**

I have three brothers. Dylan has _____________ hair and a

_____________ grin. Blair has _____________ hair than Dylan and a

_____________ grin. Nicholas has the _____________ hair of all three and the

_____________ grin.

Instead of adding *er* or *est* to an adjective when we compare things, we use *more* or *most* before some adjectives; e.g. beautiful, *more* beautiful, *most* beautiful.

2. Finish the table below, changing the adjectives by adding *er, est, more* or *most*.

(a)	tidy		
(b)		more famous	
(c)			narrowest
(d)	horrible		
(e)			most wonderful

3. Use each adjective in a sentence.

(a) stronger

____

(b) funniest

____

(c) most beautiful

____

Adverbs – 1

> **Words telling how, when or where things happen are called _adverbs_.**

1. (a) Read about the two opposite people.

> *My dad and his brother, Dave, are very different. When they were young, Dave played the piano and **sang** beautifully, while Dad **sang** woefully. Dad enjoyed sport and **played** enthusiastically, but Dave hated sport and **played** reluctantly. Unlike Dad, who could **run** swiftly and **kick** and **catch** balls easily, he **ran** slowly and **kicked** and **caught** balls awkwardly. In class, Dad **wrote** neatly, but Dave **wrote** carelessly and his work was untidy. However, Dave loved art. He **worked** patiently and could **draw** and **paint** perfectly, while Dad **worked** quickly and **painted** messily. How more opposite could two boys be?*

   (b) The words in bold are verbs. Underline the adverbs telling how each of these things was done.

2. Change the highlighted adjectives into adverbs telling how something happened. The first one has been done as an example.

   (a) Dave was a **beautiful** singer. He sang ____beautifully____.

   (b) Dad was a **woeful** singer. He sang _______________.

   (c) Dad was an **enthusiastic** sportsman. He played sport _______________.

   (d) Dave was a **careless** writer. He wrote _______________.

   (e) Dave was a **patient** worker. He worked _______________.

   (f) Dad was a **messy** painter. He painted _______________.

3. Rewrite each sentence by changing the adverb so it now tells the opposite of when each thing happened.

   (a) Dave arrived at school earlier.

   ____

   (b) After Dave sang he played the piano.

   ____

   (c) Dave always enjoyed sport.

   ____

Learn from Home Workbook 4   978-1-912760-64-0   www.prim-ed.com   Prim-Ed Publishing

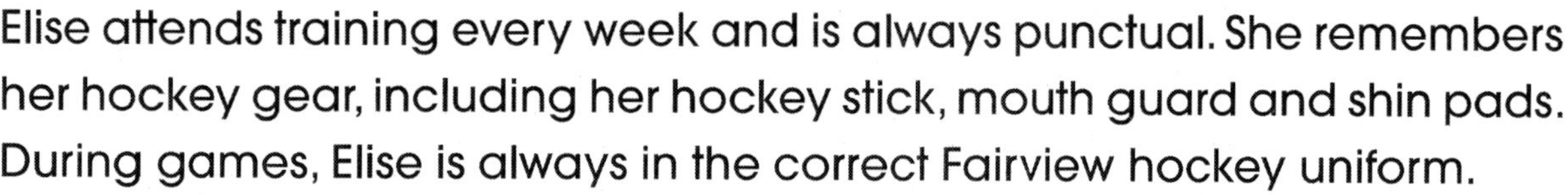

FAIRVIEW HOCKEY CLUB

Progress report – Elise Brown – mixed under 12

Elise plays hockey for the Fairview Hockey club. She is a member of the mixed under 12-year-old team.

Elise attends training every week and is always punctual. She remembers her hockey gear, including her hockey stick, mouth guard and shin pads. During games, Elise is always in the correct Fairview hockey uniform.

Although this is only Elise's second season playing hockey, she is learning important skills such as passing, hitting and dribbling.

Elise is gaining an understanding of the positions on the field and the player's roles in these positions. Playing left wing for two years now, Elise appears quite confident in the role. She travels with the ball down the left side of the field and passes it off to her team mates. Next season, Elise needs to work on travelling with the ball into the D and scoring goals. With confidence, Elise will be able to do this.

Elise positions herself well during short corners and is gaining some tackling skills. She is progressing well as a hockey player and continues to improve her skills.

Well done on a great season, Elise! Keep it up!

Use the report on page 39 to complete the page.

1. Title

2. Classification

(a) Elise plays hockey. True ☐ False ☐

(b) There are only girls in Elise's team. True ☐ False ☐

(c) Elise is less than 12 years old. True ☐ False ☐

3. Description

(a) How many paragraphs make up the description section of this report? 2 ☐ 3 ☐ 4 ☐ 5 ☐

(b) (i) Which paragraph has information about Elise's hockey gear? ☐

(ii) Draw and label the gear she brings to training.

(c) Circle the verbs written in the present tense.

(i) Elise plays hockey for the Fairview Hockey Club.

(ii) Elise attends training every week and is always punctual.

(d) Use a person's name (Elise) and pronouns like, 'he', 'she' and 'they' to change this sentence from the second to the third person.

You position yourself well during short corners.

(e) Add three more technical words used in the report.

mouthguard,

4. Conclusion

(a) Who do you think has written this progress report?

(b) Colour the face to show how you think this person feels about Elise's progress in hockey.

1. Think of a sport you know well. Can you name any successful athletes who play it? Write a progress report about an athlete—real or imaginary. Remember: Use the third person (he/she/they) and the present tense.

Title

Name of athlete.

General statement

Include type of sport and number of years playing.

Description

Conclusion

The final sentence(s) about the athlete.
Include your opinion about the success of the athlete in his or her sport.

2. Write your report.

3. Edit your work.

The Trojan horse

Read the recount.

Queen helen of greece was kidnapped by prince paris who took her back to his home in troy The greek people were very (upset/ubset) and sent ulysses and his warriors to troy to get their queen back

Athena, the goddess of war, told ulysses to build a huge wooden horse and to leave it outside the gates of troy The greeks (pretended/pertended) to leave troy but (instead/insted) they hid inside the huge horse

The trojans discovered the horse and (bought/brought) it into their city Believing the war was over they had a huge celebration (Afterwoods/Afterwards) when everyone was tired they all fell asleep

When all was (quiet/quite), the greeks opened the wooden horse and attacked the trojans They rescued queen helen and set (sale/sail) for their home in greece

❶ Punctuation

(a) The recount needs 18 capital letters for proper nouns and 9 full stops.

(b) Three commas are missing from paragraph 3.

❷ Spelling

(a) Circle the correct word in each bracket.

❸ Grammar

A recount is usually written in the past tense as the events have already occurred.

(a) In the text, underline the past tense of these verbs and write them below.

(to send) (to tell) (to bring)

____________ ____________ ____________

(to discover) (to open) (to rescue)

____________ ____________ ____________

(b) What is the difference between the past tense of the top three verbs and the last three verbs you wrote?

____

____

(c) From the text, list:

(i) 2 adjectives from paragraph 2.

____________ ____________

(ii) 4 common nouns from paragraph 1.

____________ ____________

____________ ____________

(iii) 1 plural noun ____________

❹ Vocabulary

(a) Write 2 synonyms (words with the same meaning) for 'huge'.

____________ ____________

Pottery houses

Read the procedure.

materials:

- *pensil*
- *paper*
- *string*
- *scewer*
- *knife*

- *sissors*
- *rolling pin*
- *a ball of clay*
- *carving tools*
- *2 flat thin pieces of wood*

instructions:

1. *roll the clay between the peices of wood until it is an even thikness*

2. *use paper about the same size as the clay to draw a house shape*

3. *cut out the house place it on the clay and trase around it with the nife remove the extra clay*

4. *use the tools or excess clay to add detail to the house shape*

5. *poke a hole near the top with the skewer*

6. *allow to dry and hang by the string to display*

❶ Punctuation

(a) The procedure needs 9 capital letters, 7 full stops and 2 commas between words in lists.

(b) Circle the colons.

❷ Spelling

(a) Seven different words are misspelt. Underline each then write the correct spelling.

____

____

____

(b) Which word needed a silent 'k'?

____

(c) Write two more silent 'k' words.

_______________   _______________

❸ Grammar

Adverbs add meaning to verbs.

(a) Write adverbs to match these verbs.

  (i)   roll   _______________________

  (ii) place _______________________

  (iii) cut   _______________________

Pronouns may be used in place of a noun. In the text, 'it' is used to mean 'the clay' or 'the house'.

(b) Write a pronoun to match each of these words:

  (i)   girl _________   (ii) boy _________

  (iii) parents _______ (iv) toy _________

❹ Writing

(a) Complete this sentence using commas to list the materials needed to make a cup of coffee.

I will need _____________________

____

_______________________________.

Monkeynaut

gordo the squirrel monkey was lornched into space by the united states Army on 13 december 1958 inside the nose-cone of a spacecraft called Jupiter AM-13 sientists wanted to see if a human being could survive a flight into space

gordo wore a speshl helmet and was strapped into a chair he had buttons and levers to press during the flight to see if he could perform jobs as well as survive the flite

gordo survived the flight but when the spacecraft touched down in the atlantic ocean he drownd because the device that was supposed to keep him ufloat did not work and sank

❶ Punctuation

(a) The recount needs 10 capital letters (8 for proper nouns), 5 full stops and 4 missing commas (2 in the first sentence and 2 in the last).

❷ Spelling

(a) Six words are misspelt. Underline them then write the correct spelling.

______________   ______________

______________   ______________

______________   ______________

❸ Grammar

Recounts use verbs in the past tense.

(a) Change the verbs from past tense to present tense.

(i)   was launched ________________

(ii) was strapped ________________

(iii) survived ________________

(iv) was supposed to ________________

____

❹ Vocabulary

(a) Write 2 compound words from the text.

____

Synonyms are words which have nearly the same meaning as another word.

(b) Write synonyms for the words below.

(i)   launched ________________

(ii) called ________________

(iii) survive ________________

(iv) perform ________________

(v) touched down ________________

Shortened forms of words and groups of words can be used.

(c) What words in the text do these shortened forms represent?

(i) Dec. ________________

(ii) US ________________

(d) Shorten these words.

(i) Road ______ (ii) kilometre ______

ROUNDING NUMBERS TO 10

1. Round these numbers to the nearest 10. (Remember, numbers ending in 5 are rounded up.)

(a) 7 to _______   (b) 12 to _______   (c) 31 to _______

(d) 49 to _______   (e) 34 to _______   (f) 65 to _______

(g) 16 to _______   (h) 97 to _______   (i) 43 to _______

(j) 25 to _______   (k) 78 to _______   (l) 54 to _______

2. Colour the nearest 10 to the number underlined.

(a) (0) 4 (10)   (b) (20) 26 (30)   (c) (50) 53 (60)

(d) (40) 45 (50)   (e) (80) 82 (90)   (f) (90) 97 (100)

3. Round each number to the nearest 10 in these sums and estimate the answer;
   e.g. 8 (10) + 23 (20) = about 30.

(a) 6 (_______) + 11 (_______) = about _______

(b) 16 (_______) + 9 (_______) = about _______

(c) 19 (_______) + 15 (_______) = about _______

(d) 23 (_______) + 32 (_______) = about _______

(e) 29 (_______) – 11 (_______) = about _______

(f) 38 (_______) – 24 (_______) = about _______

(g) 61 (_______) – 26 (_______) = about _______

(h) 75 (_______) – 34 (_______) = about _______

CHALLENGE

Use a calculator to find the exact answers to the sums in Question 3.

(a) _______   (b) _______   (c) _______   (d) _______

(e) _______   (f) _______   (g) _______   (h) _______

Objective   *Rounds two-digit numbers to the nearest 10.*

ROUNDING NUMBERS TO 100

1. Round these numbers to the nearest 100. (Remember, numbers ending in 50 are rounded up.)

   (a) 32 to _______   (b) 120 to _______   (c) 411 to _______

   (d) 294 to _______   (e) 350 to _______   (f) 658 to _______

   (g) 167 to _______   (h) 973 to _______   (i) 743 to _______

   (j) 825 to _______   (k) 648 to _______   (l) 554 to _______

2. Colour the nearest 100 to the number underlined.

   (a) (0) 39 (100)   (b) (200) 263 (300)   (c) (600) 650 (700)

   (d) (400) 445 (500)   (e) (900) 982 (1000)   (f) (800) 817 (900)

3. Round each number to the nearest 100 in these sums and estimate the answer;
   e.g. 312 (300) + 279 (300) = about 600.

   (a) 345 (_______) + 119 (_______) = about _______

   (b) 168 (_______) + 79 (_______) = about _______

   (c) 419 (_______) + 250 (_______) = about _______

   (d) 299 (_______) + 538 (_______) = about _______

   (e) 923 (_______) – 412 (_______) = about _______

   (f) 704 (_______) – 656 (_______) = about _______

   (g) 750 (_______) – 325 (_______) = about _______

   (h) 803 (_______) – 467 (_______) = about _______

CHALLENGE

Use a calculator to find the exact answers to the sums in Question 3.

(a) _______   (b) _______   (c) _______   (d) _______

(e) _______   (f) _______   (g) _______   (h) _______

Objective   *Rounds three-digit numbers to the nearest 100.*

ADDITION WORD PROBLEMS

1. Read, set out and solve these addition word problems.

(a) There are 24 birds in one aviary and 15 in another. 14 eggs hatch so there are 14 babies. How many birds are there altogether?		(d) There are 28 books on the top shelf, 19 on the middle and 24 on the bottom. How many books are there altogether?	
(b) There were 3 trees with 18, 21 and 32 oranges. How many oranges were there altogether?		(e) Chloe has 24 pencils, Liana 18 and Jade 16. How many pencils do they have altogether?	
(c) Tania travels 32 km by train, 16 km by bus and 5 km by taxi to get to the city. How many kilometres does she travel altogether?		(f) There are 4 dogs. Each has pups; the first 3, the second 5, the third 4 and the fourth 6. How many pups are there altogether?	

2. Write your own addition word problems for these sums.

(a) $12 + 9 + 20 =$ _________

(b) $67 + 38 + 21 =$ _________

CHALLENGE

Check your answers. Tick (✔) them if they are correct and cross (✗) them if they are incorrect. Rework any incorrect solutions.

Objective *Calculates and solves addition word problems.*

MEASURING IN SQUARE CENTIMETRES

Area can be measured in square centimetres (cm²).

1. Find the area of the shapes below by counting the centimetre squares.

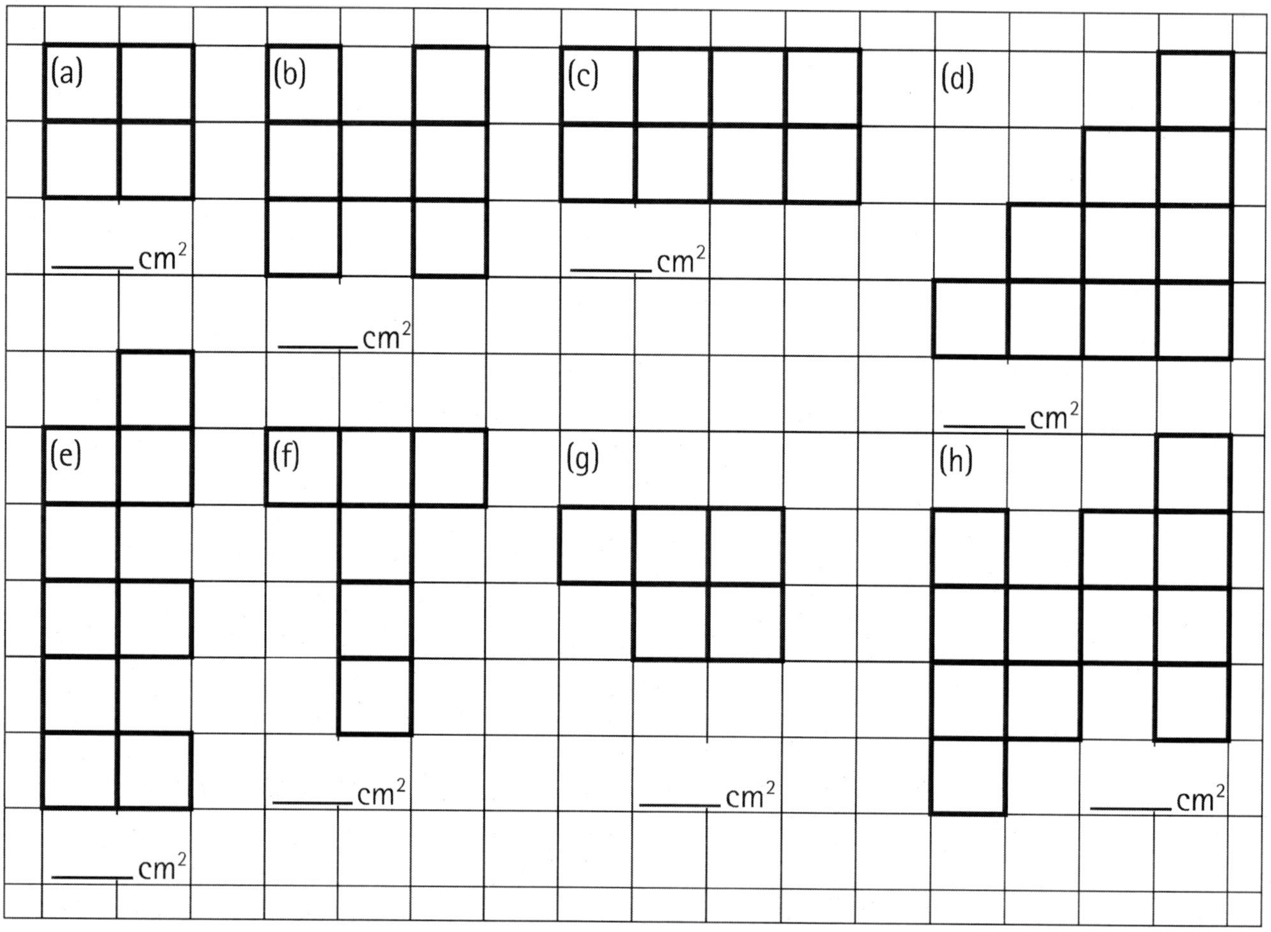

(a) _____ cm²   (b) _____ cm²   (c) _____ cm²   (d) _____ cm²

(e) _____ cm²   (f) _____ cm²   (g) _____ cm²   (h) _____ cm²

2. Order the shapes from the smallest to the largest.

_____ , _____ , _____ , _____ , _____ , _____ , _____ , _____ .

3. Trace an object of your choice below. Count the whole grid squares only to find its area.

Area = _____ cm²

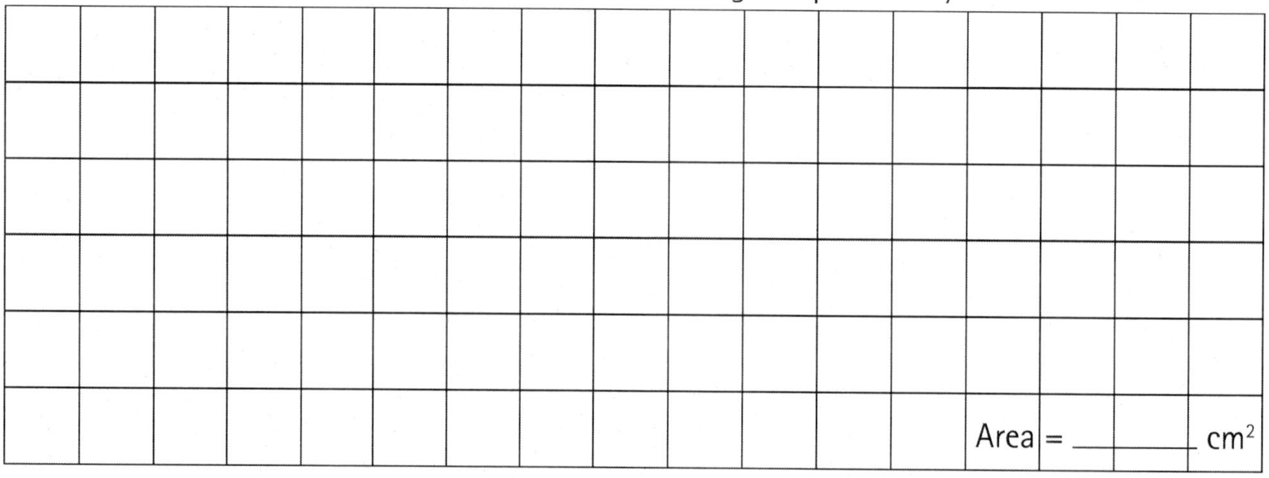

CHALLENGE Trace your foot onto 1-cm grid paper and count the whole squares only to find its area. Area = _________ cm²

Objective   *Measures areas of shapes using square centimetres.*

AREA AND PERIMETER

1. Find the area and perimeter of these shapes. Count the inside squares to find the area and the squares around the edge of the shape to find the perimeter.

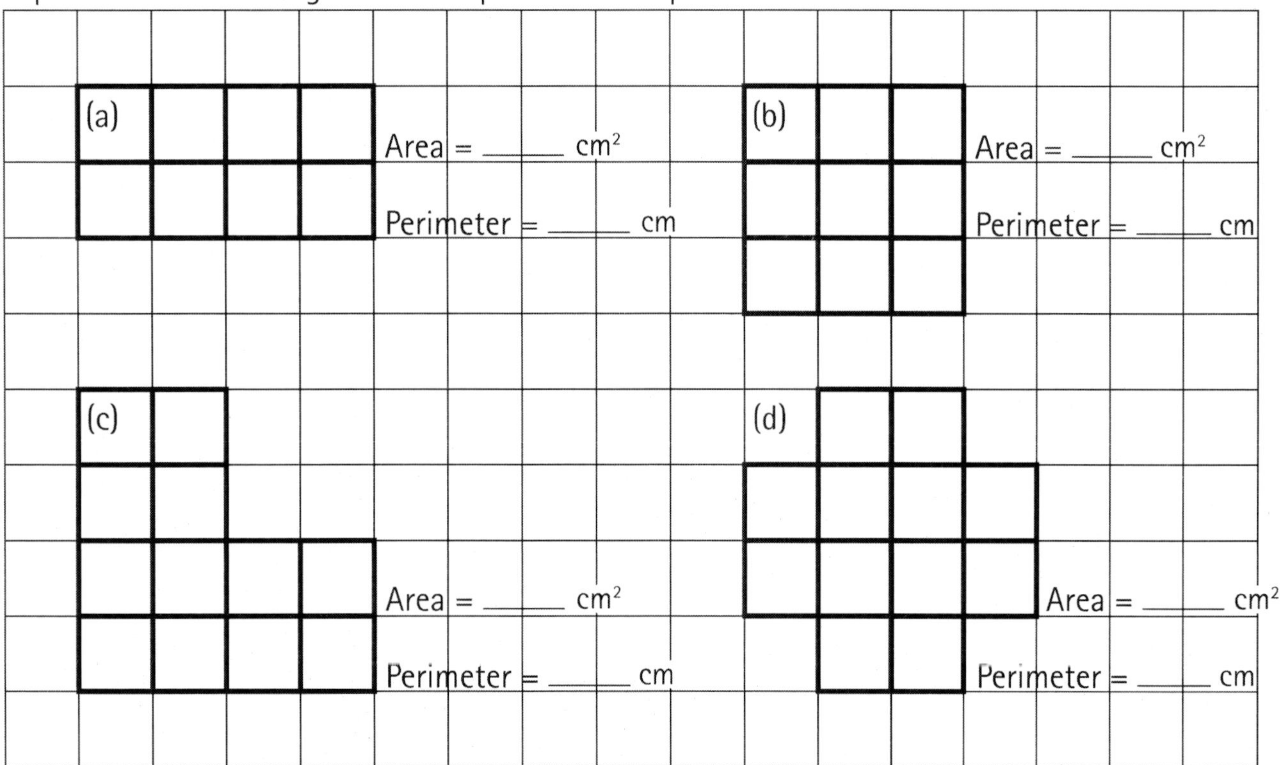

(a) Area = _______ cm²

Perimeter = _______ cm

(b) Area = _______ cm²

Perimeter = _______ cm

(c) Area = _______ cm²

Perimeter = _______ cm

(d) Area = _______ cm²

Perimeter = _______ cm

2. Trace one hand below (fingers together). Then count the whole inside squares to find its area and the outside squares to find its perimeter.

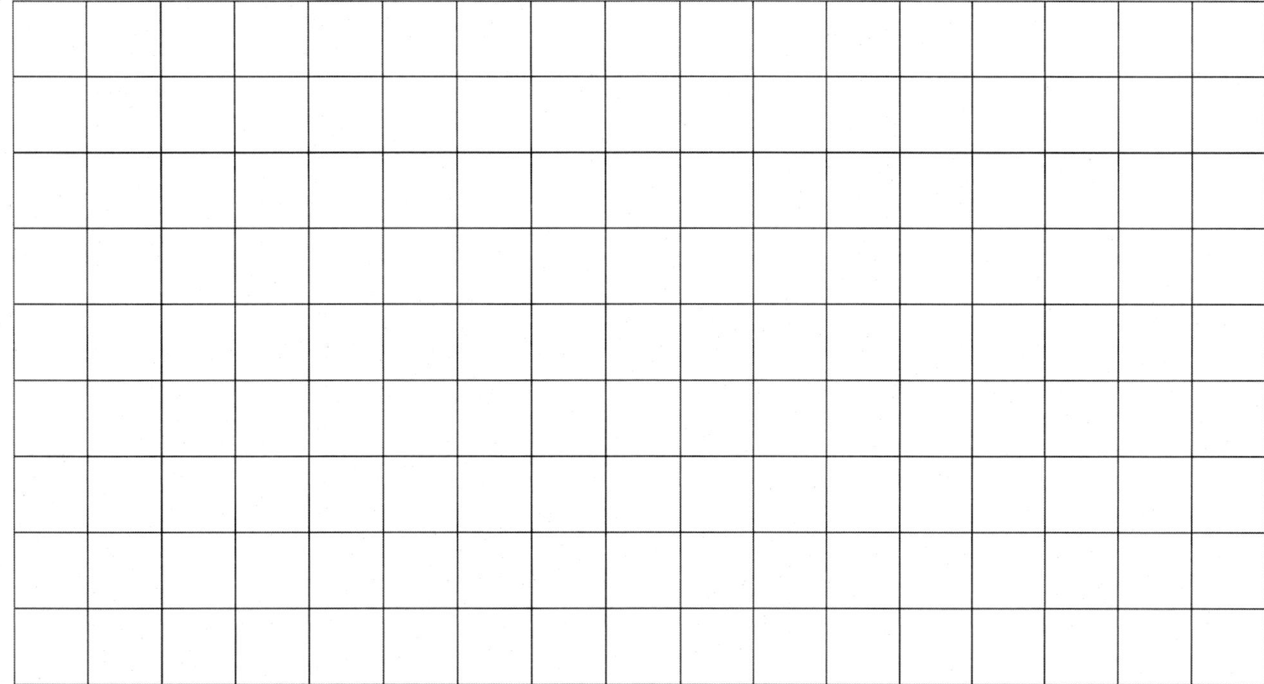

CHALLENGE

Use cubes to find the area and perimeter of a dictionary.

Area = _________ cubes. Perimeter = _________ cubes.

Objective   *Measures the area and perimeter of shapes.*

ORDERING ANGLES

1. Make these angles using lolly sticks and label them correctly: 45°, 90°, 180°.
   Tick when you have completed each model.

   (a) completed ☐   (b) completed ☐   (c) completed ☐

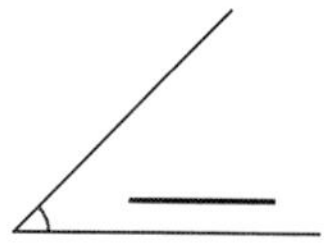

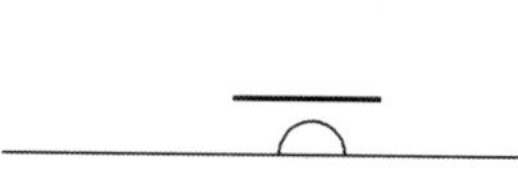

A line that has travelled in a complete circle has a 360° angle.

2. Order these angles from the smallest (1) to the largest (4).

   (a)   (b)   (c)   (d)

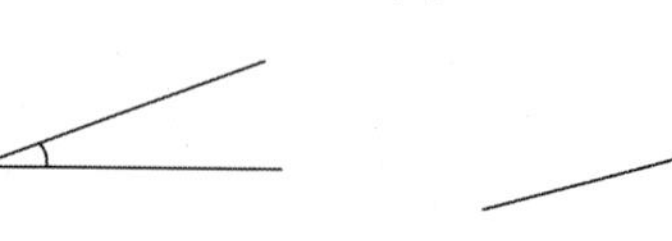
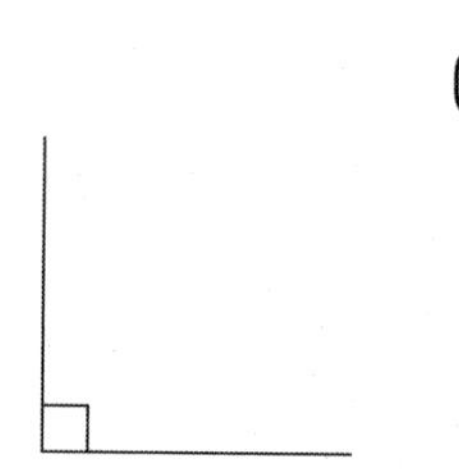

   ☐   ☐   ☐   ☐

3. Order these angles from the largest (1) to the smallest (4).

   (a)   (b)   (c)   (d)

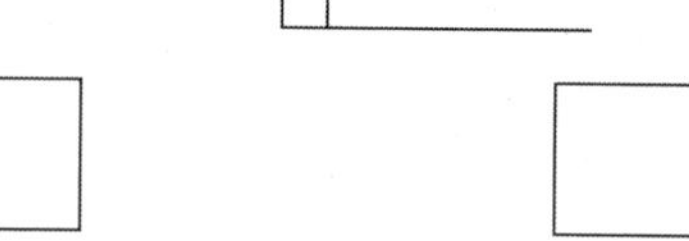
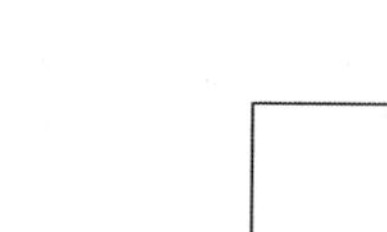

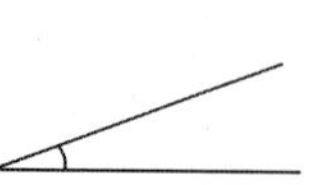
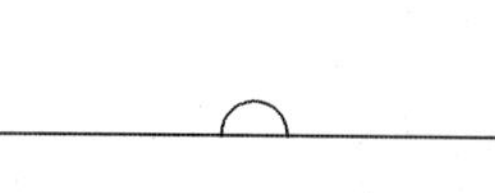
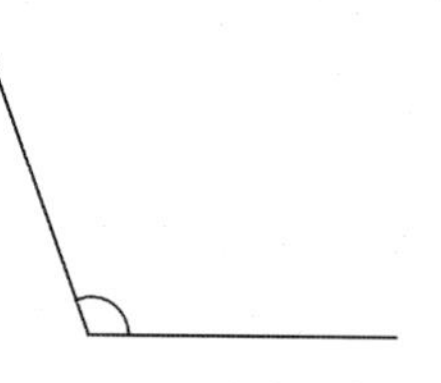
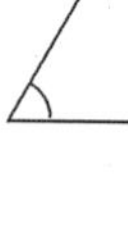

   ☐   ☐   ☐   ☐

CHALLENGE

Write the names of two shapes that have ...

(a) right angles _________________ and _________________

(b) angles smaller than right angles _________________ and _________________

(c) angles larger than right angles _________________ and _________________

Objective   *Orders sets of angles.*

CLASSIFYING ANGLES

1. Trace over the 90° angles, circle those less than 90° and draw a cross on those greater than 90°.

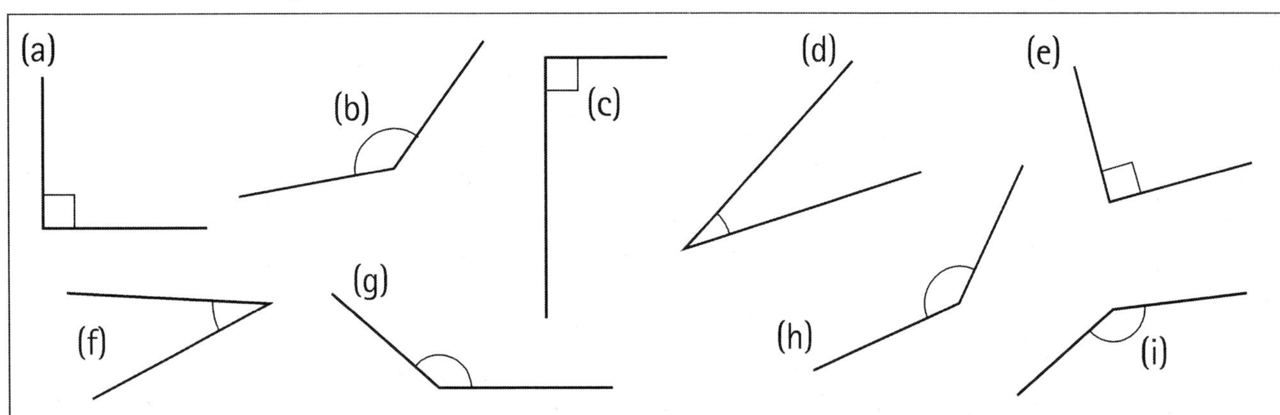

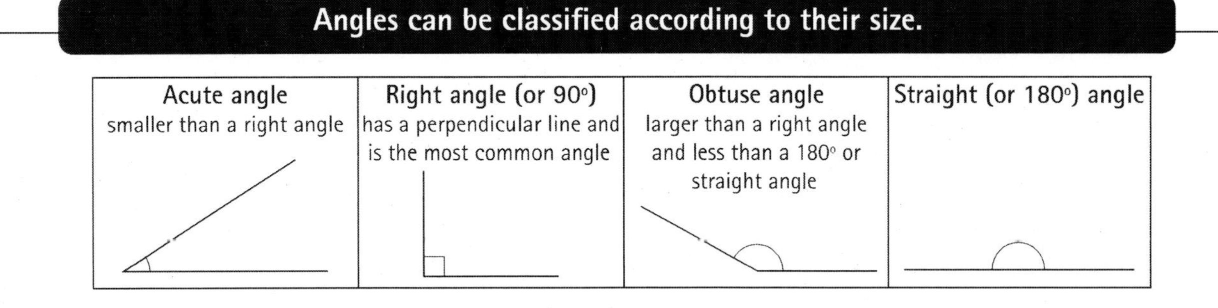

2. Colour the shapes that have:

   (a) right angles red.

   (b) acute angles yellow.

   (c) obtuse angles blue.

   (Note: one shape will need to be two colours.)

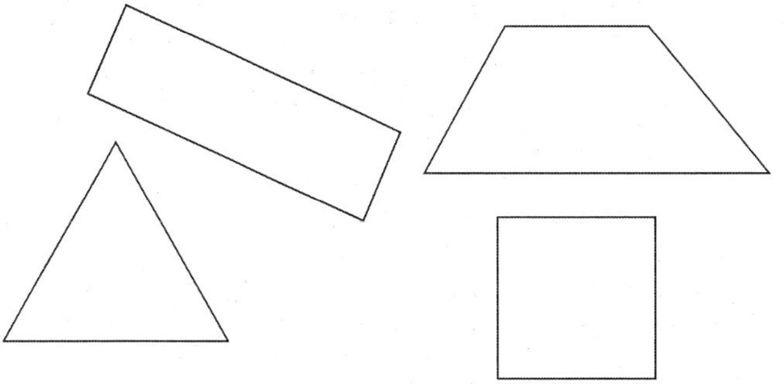

3. Find and name the angles you can see in the classroom.

   (a) Right angles

   ____

   ____

   (b) Straight angles

   ____

   ____

   (c) Acute angles

   ____

   ____

   (d) Obtuse angles

   ____

   ____

CHALLENGE On the back of this sheet, draw one shape that has:

(a) an acute angle   (b) a right angle   (c) an obtuse angle

Objective *Identifies and classifies different angles.*

Minibeast hunt

Draw and write about two minibeasts you found on your hunt.

What was it doing?

What does it look like?

Name

Where was it found?

When did you find it?

What was it doing?

What does it look like?

Name

Where was it found?

When did you find it?

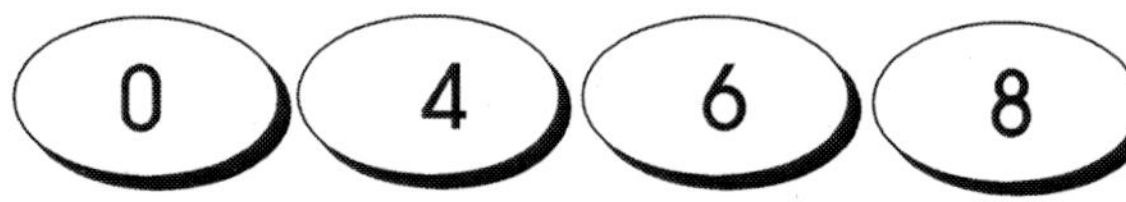

Look carefully at your minibeast and complete the questions below.

1 Number of legs.

0   4   6   8

Words that describe.

____

____

2 Number of body parts.

0   4   6   8

Words that describe.

____

____

3 Eyes

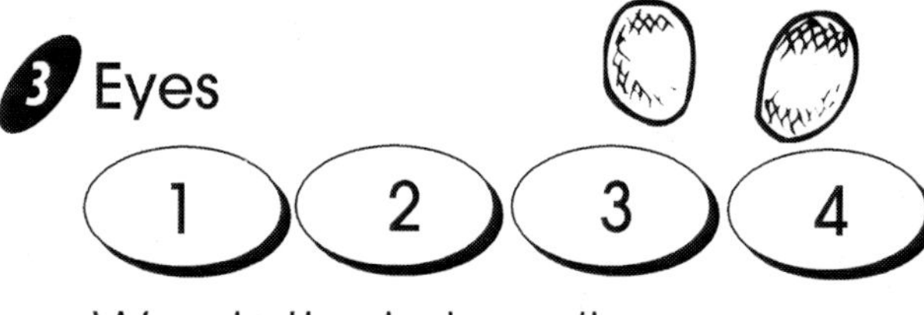

1   2   3   4

Words that describe.

____

____

4 Antennae

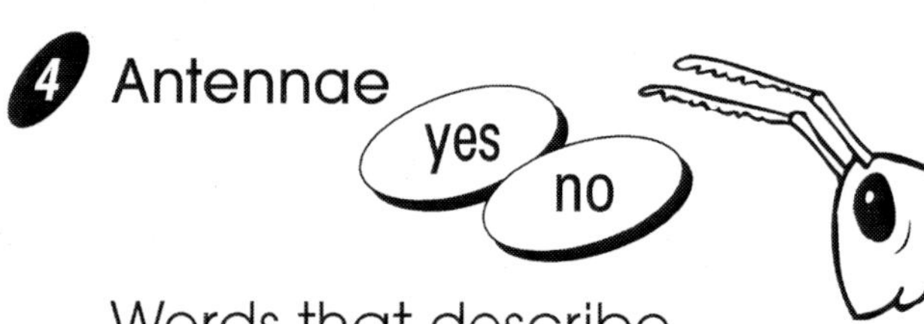

Words that describe.

____

____

5 How does your minibeast move? ______________________

____

6 Special features. ______________________

____

Draw and label your minibeast.

Saving water

1 If water was no longer available from our taps, what might happen? List two things that could happen.

(a) _______________________________________

(b) _______________________________________

2 Look at these water-saving ideas. Add some of your own.

Fix leaking taps.

Take shorter showers.

Install a rainwater tank.

Use full loads in the washing machine.

Turn off the tap when you brush your teeth.

Rinse dishes in a bowl or sink (not under running tap).

3 Design a poster with lots of water-saving ideas. Use your own drawings or cut out pictures from magazines. Plan your poster below.

Learn from Home Workbook 4   978-1-912760-64-0   www.prim-ed.com   Prim-Ed Publishing

All about recycling

To recycle means to use again or make into something different.

1 Use these words to complete this passage about recycling.

new	shredded	Empty	worms	cans

(a) Old bottles can be melted down and remade into

_______________ bottles.

(b) Used paper can be _______________ and made into new paper.

(c) Tin cans can be melted and made into new _______________.

(d) _______________ plastic bottles can be cleaned and made into new plastic bottles.

(e) Kitchen scraps can be fed to _______________ or hens.

2 Materials have to be prepared for recycling. Draw pictures to show the process.

(a) Glass: rinse out, clean and remove lid.

(b) Paper: remove any metal bits (staples), stack newspapers together and tie in a bundle.